# LIVE Fully.
# LEAD Authentically.

**The Surprising Link Between Self-Awareness and Your Impact**

**KURT BUSH** AND **CHRIS GODFREDSEN**

Live Fully Lead Authentically: Engaging the Power of the Brimstone Coaching Equation E+R=T to Transform Your Life and Leadership
Copyright © 2025 Kurt Bush and Chris Godfredsen

All rights reserved.

No part of this book may be reproduced, stored, or transmitted by any means—whether auditory, graphic, mechanical, or electronic—without written permission of both publisher and author, except in the case of brief excerpts used in critical articles and reviews. Unauthorized reproduction of any part of this work is illegal and is punishable by law.

Scripture quotations are taken from the Holy Bible, New International Version®, NIV®. Copyright © 1973, 1978, 1984, 2011 by Biblica, Inc.™ Used by permission of Zondervan. All rights reserved worldwide. www.zondervan.com The "NIV" and "New International Version" are trademarks registered in the United States Patent and Trademark Office by Biblica, Inc.™

Published by BCG Publishing
Rock Valley, Iowa
https://www.brimstonecoachinggroup.com/

Cover Design by IMMIX Marketing
Interior Formatting by Inspire Books

Print ISBN: 979-8-9988185-0-9
e-book ISBN: 979-8-9988185-1-6
Library of Congress: 2025910499

Please note that *we* don't make any guarantees about the results of the information applied within this content. *We* share educational and informational resources that are intended to help you succeed in your own transformational journey. You nevertheless need to know that your ultimate success or failure will be the result of your own efforts, your particular situation, and innumerable other circumstances beyond *our* knowledge and control.

Printed in the United States

"Chris and Kurt are trusted friends who embody the very journey they invite us into—one marked by honesty, courage, and grace. *Live Fully Lead Authentically* offers a clear, compassionate framework for transformation rooted in both practical coaching wisdom and deep personal experience. It's not just about better leadership; it's about becoming whole. For anyone ready to stop white-knuckling their way through life and start leading from a truer self, this book is a trusted companion."

—**Chuck DeGroat, PhD,** Professor of Pastoral Care & Christian Spirituality, Executive Director, Clinical Mental Health Counseling Program, Licensed Professional Counselor, Michigan, Author, *When Narcissism Comes to Church*

"I love this book and the powerful concepts and tools that are described in it. If you want a better life, buy it, read it, apply it!"

—**Rodger Price**, Founder and Partner, Leading by DESIGN

"As I'm finishing my PhD, creating psychologically safe spaces has become central to my organizational belief system—AND my personal belief system. Chris and Kurt illuminate ways to find that safety to be the best version of ourselves. With their game-changing equation and experience working with leaders like you and me, this work is transformational and worth every minute you invest in it."

—**Tyler Reagin**, Leadership Author, Consultant, Speaker, Co-founder, 10TEN Project, Owner, The Life-Giving Company

"Imagine you're facing a daunting task—your own messy life. You roll up your sleeves and get to work. Now, picture two guys coming alongside you, offering calm encouragement and handing you effective tools, one after the other, just when you need them. Before long, your toolbox is full, and you're growing more confident that you'll have what you need when you need it. These tools consist of information, insights and personal stories—each one fitting perfectly in your hand. Eventually, you receive a belt for these tools—a formula called E + R = T. This brings everything together, ensuring you have all you need. Before you know it, you're making progress on your big job and enjoying it too.

This is how I experienced *Live Fully Lead Authentically* by Chris Godfredsen and Kurt Bush. I've known them for years, and they are the real deal when it comes to doing their own work on their lives and then describing their learning for others to use."

—**Trisha Taylor**, The Leader's Journey

"In an age when we find ourselves facing a crisis of leadership on so many levels, Kurt Bush and Chris Godfredsen offer a vision and model for transformational leadership that goes beyond slick technique and quick fixes. As someone who knows both of these authors well, I can assure you that they're 'the real deal,' not just offering content in the abstract but sharing with us lessons learned and wisdom gained from their own personal work of deep change. The book you hold in your hands is a gift, and the authors are trustworthy guides! I highly recommend *Live Fully Lead Authentically*, not just for your own growth but for your team and other leaders with whom you might engage the insights and practices found in this incredibly helpful book. Prepare to be changed!"

—**Rev. Dr. Brian Keepers**, Lead Pastor, Trinity Reformed Church (Orange City & Hospers, IA)

# CONTENTS

Acknowledgments . . . . . . . . . . . . . . . . . . . . . . . . . . v
Foreword . . . . . . . . . . . . . . . . . . . . . . . . . . . . . . . xi
Introduction . . . . . . . . . . . . . . . . . . . . . . . . . . . . xiii

**Chapter 1**   The Transformational Journey . . . . . . . . . . . . . . 1
**Chapter 2**   Why Do We Do This Work? . . . . . . . . . . . . . 9
**Chapter 3**   The Transformational Equation . . . . . . . . . . . 21
**Chapter 4**   Promises, Promises, Promises . . . . . . . . . . . . 38
**Chapter 5**   Welcoming All Parts of Yourself . . . . . . . . . . . 64
**Chapter 6**   Once You See It, You Can't Unsee It . . . . . . . . . . 74
**Chapter 7**   Agency . . . . . . . . . . . . . . . . . . . . . . . . . . 78
**Chapter 8**   Why the Transformational Journey Matters . . . . . . 83
**Chapter 9**   A Word About Resilience . . . . . . . . . . . . . . 110

Epilogue . . . . . . . . . . . . . . . . . . . . . . . . . . . . . . . 117
About the Authors . . . . . . . . . . . . . . . . . . . . . . . . . 119

# ACKNOWLEDGMENTS

**CHRIS**

I had my first introduction to Murray Bowen's family systems theory in an extended unit of clinical pastoral education (CPE) at St. Luke's Hospital in Sioux City, Iowa, more than fifteen years ago now, under the watchful eye of Rev. Steve Pullman.

Sitting in a room with Pullman, Rev. Jon Millen (another CPE facilitator), and several other students opened my eyes to the work of self-awareness for the very first time.

I was not a very curious person. I had been taught right and wrong by my parents as a child. Various coaches throughout my adolescent and college years taught me more life lessons, and one of the most meaningful encounters in my life occurred in the student center at the small college I attended.

Nearing the end of my college years, one of my baseball coaches, Mark Bloemendaal, sat me down and asked me this question: "How do you want to be remembered around here?" He then proceeded to tell me how people saw me—not from a place of shame but rather from a place of love. He genuinely cared about me.

That question made its way in and out of my consciousness for years before it finally registered around the age of thirty-six. Now, twenty years later, I see that as a marker in my life.

Another marker was the day I met Steve Pullman, but I need to back up just a bit. I met Steve Pullman because of the grace extended to me by my wife, Kathy. In fact, I credit her transformational journey as the impetus for mine. As I began to see her behaving in new ways, I began to get curious.

Kathy and I had been married for a number of years, and though our business and family life were chaotic, she consented to my pursuit of additional learning. That learning would eventually benefit our marriage and our relationship because I actually began asking questions. We got to know each other in profound ways because of my increased curiosity, and we even began to argue differently—all of which was a wonderful side benefit of the journey.

CPE wrecked me—in a good way. Through writing verbatims, processing some of my deeply held beliefs and where they came from, and getting to process my experience of caring for patients at Mercy and St. Luke's Hospitals, I was exposed to a realm I hadn't been previously aware of.

The same was true for meeting Rodger Price, who founded Leading by DESIGN in 2014. He built his business on the premise that leadership skills are not always inherent, but when those skills are offered through experiential and reinforced learning models, they can be developed. Before founding Leading by DESIGN, Rodger was the coach of the coaches in the Reformed Church in America (RCA) and was my first coach in a professional setting. The impact Rodger has had on my life cannot be overstated.

From there, my transformational journey afforded me the opportunity to meet Jim Herrington and Trisha Taylor. These two, along with Western Theological Seminary and the RCA, facilitated and coached a transformational learning process that is now known as Churches Learning Change. I was immersed in the CLC world for a number of years and am indebted to Jim and Trisha.

One component of the Churches Learning Change process is an ongoing process of spiritual formation known as Faithwalking. Jim and Trisha were instrumental in the early iterations of Faithwalking and were kind and patient with me as I learned and grew both with and from them. Jim and Trisha now lead one of the nation's preeminent coaching practices, The Leader's Journey, and have authored a book by the same name.

As Ken Shuman took over as the executive director of Faithwalking, he reworked much of the curriculum into six ten-week modules known as Faithwalking Foundations. And, of them all, Ken has had the most profound impact on my life when I think about Family Systems Theory, understanding and managing anxiety, and so much of what you will read in the pages that follow. Ken and I have built a special friendship over the past decade, and I'm eternally grateful for the ways he has coached, listened, and shown me the way in this work.

Faithwalking and the aforementioned learning have helped to shape our work at Brimstone Coaching Group in profound ways. Kurt and I still facilitate and coach Faithwalking modules and encourage everyone who will give us ten minutes to engage in that transformational process.

Each of these people, and countless others, have shaped what you are about to read. In addition, Kurt, Jamie, Michael, and Brian have been blessings on this journey, and so have countless others who have participated in Faithwalking modules I have led and coached, as well as workshops that Brimstone Coaching Group has facilitated. Steve and Leanne, you are among those I owe a debt of gratitude.

## KURT

As Chris highlighted above for himself, I, too, was not a very curious person for a very long time. For most of my early adulthood, I was a very black-and-white thinker. I knew what was "right," and I got stirred up and defensive when I felt that someone was out of line with what was "right."

The earliest conversation that began to cause a shift in me was with my friend Luke at Hall of Fame Pizza and Wings in Dewitt, Iowa. Luke and I worked in the same manufacturing plant together, and on this particular day, we decided to go to lunch together. While there, we began talking about a recent—and rather large—action taken by a governmental agency. I was extremely stirred up and defensive, likely coming across as though I thought the proverbial sky was falling. It sure felt that way.

Luke was not stirred up. In fact, I so clearly to this day remember thinking, "Geez, Luke, why don't you care about this stuff?!" Luke did care. But he wasn't anxious about it. He asked me this simple question: "What difference does this make in your daily life?" I couldn't answer.

Of course, it's OK to care about things that don't impact our daily lives. We should. But what that question—and my inability to answer—showed me was that I was not in control of my response to that government action (among other things), and I didn't like it.

From there, Western Theological Seminary continued normalizing the work of self-discovery, self-awareness, and even therapy. For the first time, these things were not only offered as an option but encouraged as part of the process of becoming a whole human. The five years I spent in that system were hugely formative in so many ways. Thank you, WTS faculty and staff!

I owe a debt of gratitude to my coauthor, Chris, for inviting me into the Faithwalking process early in my time at WTS. I had no idea the impact Faithwalking would have. It was immense. Chris, thanks for not taking my initial "no" all those years ago. Faithwalking, as Chris alluded to, continues to be a really beautiful part of my life even today. It's a gift to welcome others into the journey that has meant so much to me.

In December 2019, I began serving a multi-campus church alongside Brian Keepers. Brian is THE least anxious leader I have ever met or observed. If you remember, 2020 was a little chaotic. Not only was there the global COVID-19 pandemic, but at the same time, the denomination we served in was imploding in ways that are still difficult to wrap my head around. Brian, you taught me so much about leadership, specifically the idea that leaders lead by doing their own work to become the least anxious, most curious presence in any situation. I'm grateful for all that you modeled for me.

That same church was the first organization I'd ever worked for that seriously invested in me—not in the form of salary or perks or anything like that, but in the form of a really great coach (dare I say one of THE preeminent leadership coaches today). Jim Herrington was my first formal leadership coach, and it fundamentally changed how I view leadership. Jim, you not only taught me that leadership is how I grow myself and how I navigate all the things in me (not some authoritarian leadership where the leader knows all the things) but you also unknowingly taught me how to coach others. My time with you helped me uncover how much I love not only engaging in this work for myself but how much I love helping others do the same for themselves. I am here—and BCG is here—because of your example and coaching. Thank you doesn't seem like strong enough language but THANK YOU!

My wife, Amber, has been through a lot. Years of seminary, years of Faithwalking work, years of transformation, and, of course, the formation of the Brimstone Coaching Group. Neither of us today is who we were when we were first married—in all the best ways. You've extended so much grace to me as that transformation happened and as BCG has taken shape. Thank you, and I love you!

Joel and Pam: You two have been an important part of my life for nearly twenty years. I am so grateful for you both and for the relationship we share. You're amazing friends and even better cheerleaders. Thank you!

As I write this, I'm present to the fact that you all are such critical pieces of the puzzle that make up my life that have led to the content in the coming pages. Know that your influence and impact are all over every single page of this book!

# FOREWORD

It's a rare and refreshing thing to encounter a book that is as honest, practical, and deeply rooted in lived experience as *Live Fully, Lead Authentically*. My friends and colleagues Kurt Bush and Chris Godfredsen have offered a gem of a resource for personal growth and transformation. This isn't a collection of theories or abstract principles. This is the fruit of personal transformation, tested in the fires of real life and refined through years of coaching others through their own journeys.

Chris and Kurt are not writing from the safety of the sidelines. They are speaking as fellow travelers—people who have done the hard work of transformation themselves. I've had the privilege of walking alongside both of them for years now, and I've watched their personal growth unfold in real time. The transformation they describe in these pages is not theoretical. I've seen it up close—slow, steady, hard-won, and deeply authentic.

As you read their stories, and those of the clients they have faithfully served, you'll sense the depth of their integrity. They don't pretend this work is easy. It's not. But they also don't waver in their conviction that it's possible—and worth it.

What sets this book apart is its remarkable balance between insight and action. Chris and Kurt bring together some of the most important discoveries from the past generation's explosion of learning in emotional intelligence and adult development, and they combine that with their deeply rooted theological convictions. Remarkably, they translate that learning into steps you can actually take. Whether they're unpacking the role of "protective promises," teaching you to identify your internal parts through IFS (Internal Family Systems), or walking you through the practical power of their "Transformational Equation," they consistently offer grounded wisdom and actionable practices.

If you've ever found yourself wondering why you react the way you do in high-stakes moments, or if you've been frustrated with patterns you can't seem to shake, this book is for you. If you've longed to move from surviving to thriving—not just as a leader, but as a whole person—this book is for you.

The truth is, transformation is both deeply personal and profoundly communal. We need guides. We need encouragement. And we need trustworthy companions who can remind us we're not alone. Chris and Kurt offer exactly that. Through their company, The Brimstone Coaching Group, they've built a coaching practice that offers support and accountability for people who are ready to grow. I've had the privilege of working closely with them, and I hold a high level of confidence in their integrity, their wisdom, and their skill.

So take a deep breath. Settle in. What you're holding in your hands is more than a book—it's an invitation. An invitation to wholeness, to clarity, and to freedom. Chris and Kurt will be with you every step of the way. And I promise, if you're willing to engage, the journey will change you.

Welcome. You're in the right place.

—Jim Herrington, *The Leader's Journey*

# INTRODUCTION

Bruce has lived a long and successful life.

From an early age, it was clear to people around Bruce that there was something special about him. He was a good athlete, and he was an exceptional pitcher. Bruce parlayed his ability and golden left arm into a successful high school career that resulted in a college baseball scholarship.

Bruce's baseball success grew in him a desire to help others experience some of the same success he enjoyed. This desire led Bruce into a career in education. As it turned out, Bruce not only loved coaching but was a pretty good coach, too, and enjoyed a lot of success in that arena.

Later in life, Bruce arrived at the realization that coaching is a young man's game, so he left education for the world of business and finance. Again, Bruce enjoyed success and helped others succeed in reaching their business and financial dreams.

From the outside looking in, he appears to have enjoyed more success than most people have in a variety of areas. It seems like everything Bruce touched has flourished! Bruce would even acknowledge the truth of that statement, and yet, Bruce also lives with the crippling belief that he doesn't matter.

---

Elizabeth is living in the prime of her life.

She is attractive, funny, intelligent, and a quick wit. People follow Elizabeth's lead. She is often the center of attention. Whether it is in the classroom, the cafeteria, the dorm, or the gym, Elizabeth is surrounded by people who pay close attention to the things she does.

Elizabeth is also a gifted athlete, and she is jacked! Elizabeth lives in the weight room, and at twenty-one years of age, the future is bright. She enjoys her role on the college track team and aspires to compete well into adulthood.

While she knows she is more than what she does and how she performs, Elizabeth will not be outworked. Yes, genetics play a part in a person's physique, but so does close attention to diet and exercise. She spends hour after hour in the weight room—both in season and in the off-season—and even more hours on the track.

These things help fuel Elizabeth's commitment and contribute to her success, but they are not the only motivating factors. Elizabeth's commitment is also fueled by her father's lack of commitment.

---

Kevin is one tough hombré. It wasn't always true, but it is now.

Kevin doesn't have a relationship with his family of origin, at least not much of one. He and his father don't speak. He speaks to him through his mother occasionally and has little to no relationship with his brothers either.

Kevin's family didn't have much money growing up. In fact, Kevin would say his family was poor. Kids being kids, Kevin was often picked on by the other boys for not having much. Dressed in hand-me-downs and second-hand clothing, other kids often made it their mission to make Kevin's life miserable, physically beating him up when the opportunity presented itself.

As he grew, Kevin played football and became a black belt in Taekwondo. Eventually, people stopped beating up Kevin. He not only protected himself—he became the person who protected others.

Kevin would later marry and they would raise their children together. He successfully put those three boys through college, debt-free, and enveloped them into his successful business.

Despite the challenges of his childhood, he has made his mark in the world. He lives in a beautiful home overlooking the mountains, but it has all come at a cost. In fact, Kevin might even say he isn't really living. It's likely that Kevin might say, "I'm simply a passenger in life. I make sure everyone is safe and enjoys their lives."

---

There is nothing Lucy can't do. Whatever she puts her mind to, Lucy conquers.

One of six children, Lucy grew up in a family where failure was not an option. She was raised to excel in the classroom, to excel in her work, and to excel in maintaining the upstanding and proud reputation of the family.

The standards were high, and no matter how high the bar was set, Lucy cleared the bar each and every time.

This "way of being" served Lucy well. She and her husband raised a family, and their kids now have their own kids. In some ways, Lucy raised her children in the same way she was raised. In other ways, she did not, and, truth be told, that reality impacts Lucy.

Some of the things that were true to Lucy are not true for her children. The reality is they have made their own decisions and are living life the way they choose to live it. While her parents have long since passed away, Lucy wonders what they would say about her life today. That bar to be cleared still feels quite present.

---

Bill is the best!

He is empathetic. He is friendly. He is kind. There is no one Bill does not like, and there is no one who doesn't like Bill.

He is a gentle, loving, and warm soul. He is loved by his bride, his daughters, and their dogs. He is loved by his coworkers, his employers, and everyone who knows him.

Bill pastors a large church, oversees the leadership team, and manages other staff at the church. He does all these things to the best of his ability.

One thing that's true for Bill is he will do whatever it takes to do his job well. And there's a reason that goes beyond Bill simply wanting to do a good job in his work. While it was never true, there was a time in his childhood when Bill was made to believe he was not good enough. While he was not yet fully developed, his physical appearance was called into question. That comment left a painful and wounding mark, motivating Bill in real ways. It's at that point Bill decided he would be "the best."

---

Jack is the apple of his parents' eye.

Jack's parents willingly testify whenever they are given the opportunity to, without hesitation, to proclaim what a good boy he was growing up to be and how very proud they are of who he has become as an adult.

He was THE all-American kid. He was well-behaved, stayed out of trouble, and made his parents and grandparents proud. Jack could even sing like a canary and spent his summers with his band traveling around the country.

While the dream of being a world-renowned recording artist eventually faded, Jack seemed unbothered. He settled into adulthood and landed a job as the marketing team lead for a major American company by the age of thirty-one.

Jack met Jill, they were married soon thereafter and eventually had two children. Jack and Jill moved out of their apartment in the city and found the perfect house in the burbs. While building the life he had built, Jack struggled to enjoy the life he was living because his experience as a younger version of himself led him to believe that he didn't deserve good things in life.

---

Lastly, meet Dianne. Dianne is in control.

Dianne leads a nonprofit that meets the needs of people in the inner city. The needs of the people are significant, and the clientele are some of the most challenging people on earth. Their needs are great and require highly skilled people to meet those needs.

While Dianne is in control and the person in charge, the struggle is also very real. Understanding who to hire and where to put them within the organization for maximum impact is one of her most difficult challenges. While it's true that people are being served and that her community is better because of the organization she leads, Dianne regularly questions her effectiveness.

The opinions of her employees and the people she serves often impact the way Dianne shows up at work. She does her best to maintain control over her emotions while in meetings and conflicts with staff, but there are times when her trying is futile, and her emotions get the best of her.

Dianne told herself years ago that she would not be controlled. She told herself she would not be controlled by another person, by her feelings, or by situations she found herself in. The problems with being in control and never being controlled have taken a toll.

Bruce, Elizabeth, Kevin, Liz, Bill, Jack, and Dianne all have something in common. They have something in common with one another. They have something in common with all of humanity.

They have something in common with you too.

We are all human beings, and if there is one thing human beings crave, it is stasis. Stasis is that state of being whereby equilibrium is present. These are places and spaces where things are as they should be. These are places and spaces where we feel safe. Places and spaces where we know what to expect of ourselves and others. Places and spaces in which our most core and important needs are met by those people closest to us. Places and spaces where we need not fear. It sounds really good, doesn't it?

But what is also true of human beings is that we all have encounters each and every day. From birth, we have encountered dozens, if not thousands, of experiences throughout each day that impact us. And we make meaning of those experiences, often unconsciously, and respond to those experiences automatically. That meaning helps us make sense of those encounters that just don't seem to make any sense.

Perhaps you can think of a time when you've done this. Maybe it's the time your mother or father didn't follow through with what they said they would do for you. It's possible that you could make the meaning that authority figures are not to be trusted because they will only let you down.

Or maybe you had the painful encounter of being made fun of in school for something you were wearing, like Kevin from a couple pages ago. It's likely you'd make the meaning that your clothes are embarrassing and shouldn't ever leave your drawer again.

You see the problem, don't you? The problem is that the meaning we make and assign to those encounters is often one of many meanings we could possibly make—and often not the most accurate meaning. Whether the meaning was true or not, what IS true is that we aren't always able to make the most accurate meaning in the moment of encounter.

While we all want stasis, our experiences dictate otherwise, which then brings about homeostasis, the automatic process that a living thing uses to keep its body steady on the inside while continuing to adjust to conditions on the outside.

> **In a word, we all want safety.**

In a word, we all want safety. When we feel safe, we are free to be ourselves, our *truest selves*, that person we want to be in every circumstance. When we are our truest selves, we utilize our best thinking, and we are the least anxious versions of ourselves.

For each one of us—including Bruce, Elizabeth, Kevin and the gang—there were moments in our early years when we had experiences and we instantly felt unsafe.

Imagine you are at the top of the hamster wheel. All of a sudden, something happens, and you find yourself on the bottom side of the wheel, out of control. This is when you begin to feel like the wheel is rolling you versus you rolling the wheel. You are simply a passenger on this journey. When that happens, you do everything you can to climb back to the top of the wheel where you felt safe, often to no avail.

## HOW DID WE GET HERE?

The age-old question is, "How did we get here?"

It doesn't matter if you have a PhD, run a billion-dollar industry, lead a nonprofit, run a small business, or lay landscaping blocks vocationally. Each one of you had experiences when you were children. From those experiences, you made meaning. The meaning you made may have been accurate, but it also may have been inaccurate. Accurate or inaccurate doesn't really matter at the moment.

The fact is, you made meaning, and out of desperation to get back to the top of the hamster wheel, you made a promise that was designed to protect yourself so you would have the experience of safety until you were actually safe again.

We call these *protective promises*. We've all made them. Again, these promises were often made subconsciously. From the creation of that protective promise on, the promise you made dictated your behavior.

For Bruce, when he felt the same feeling he had when his opinion first didn't matter, that protective promise kicked into high gear, trying to keep him safe. That meant that he would retreat into his shell and would not dare share his thoughts or opinions.

Elizabeth's father struggled with commitment—in his marriage, with keeping his word to Elizabeth and her siblings—and, as a result, Elizabeth made the protective promise that she would not be her dad. She would be committed to everything she did so she might feel safe.

Our resident protector, Kevin, made a similar protective promise. He worked himself to the bone, protecting his wife and sons from experiencing the same type of pain he felt. He worked and worked, protected, and provided in ways that left him exhausted, frustrated, and overloaded with the demands of the protective promise. While it worked in his childhood, it now feels as though Kevin is no longer living but simply surviving.

For Lucy, the meaning she made early in life was she had to be perfect. The protective promise she made was, "I will appear to be perfect." Her appearance, her relationships, her schoolwork, and, later, her career had to reflect that she was perfect. Into adulthood, when she didn't feel safe, Lucy did whatever it took to appear perfect.

You get the picture. Bill, Jack, and Dianne created similar protective promises from experiences they had earlier in life. We believe that this is not unique to Bruce, Elizabeth, Kevin, or Lucy, but rather, these protective promises impact all of us who call ourselves part of the human race. So to you, reader, we say what a wise guide once told us: "Welcome to the human race." You are not alone.

This is how we got here.

## WHERE ARE WE GOING?

In this book, Kurt and I (Chris) intend to share with you the deep need for and a gentle invitation into the transformational journey. We will share parts of our own journeys, and as we have done above, we will share anecdotes and stories from clients we have worked with. We intentionally change names and some of the specifics to protect the innocent, but their stories are powerful, and the degree to which they have seen transformation is inspiring.

After sharing parts of our own journey, we will explain more deeply why we engage in the transformational journey. We will help you see the impact of working two jobs (the job you get paid to do *and* the job of navigating the byproducts of your protective promises) and white-knuckling your way through life. We will share some of the things that are necessary for the journey—traits like courage, grit, and honesty. And we will share a Transformational Equation that is sure to bring about change.

The book will then explain in greater detail the power of our word. We will discuss protective promises in increased detail and also introduce you to purposeful promises and preferred promises as approaches for showing up in the world the way you desire.

As we get clear on the power of your word and the way it impacts you, we will also introduce you to the concept of welcoming all parts of yourself without shame. While purposeful promises and preferred promises are critical to the transformational journey, equally so is the work of internal family systems (IFS) developed by Dr. Richard Schwartz. Through IFS, we can identify parts of you that are doing their very best to protect you from painful first-formation experiences. We will help you recognize protector parts (managers and firefighters) who are functioning in ways to help you avoid the pain that your deepest-seeded emotions and feelings experience—the parts of you that you've exiled away to avoid pain.

Through creating, developing, and practicing our work with these promises and our ongoing IFS work, we have become increasingly convinced that this saying is true: "Once you see it, you can't unsee it." We will help you see that you have agency and are able to make decisions about who and how you want to be in the world.

Lastly, we will help you see how the transformational journey will impact you in all the places and spaces where you lead. We will provide you with the ways we see this work having noticeable and lasting differences in six different leadership conversations and show you ways you will benefit from engaging in the transformational journey.

Reader, allow us to say again: We're really glad you're here with us! It's not nothing for you to embark on your own journey of transformation with us. In fact, that might be an understatement. This is downright hard work! It can be frightening work. And spoiler alert: Transformation is a long, slow process. And we get it—in 2025, long, slow processes are not processes we're all looking to jump into. But, again, we're glad you're here.

Chris and I (Kurt) don't take lightly that you've chosen to engage in this journey with us through these pages and the content that we've poured our hearts into, or maybe you've chosen to engage with us as a coaching client. Whatever level you're engaging with us, it's an honor.

But before we go further, we want to mention that this work and this process that we're about to share with you is not some nebulous and abstract work of theory we've conjured up on a whiteboard. No, quite the opposite, in fact.

Chris and I have spent years not only crafting the content and practices you're about to read but we've also spent years doing this work ourselves with wise guides as helpers along the way. A reader of a certain age will recognize this phrase: "I'm not just the president but I'm also a client!" If you don't recognize that, go to YouTube and search for the Hair Club for Men (not a sponsor). It's an enjoyable one minute to break up your day! You're welcome.

All jokes aside, we take the sentiment of that phrase to heart. It's at the very core of the work we do together. We believe so deeply that in order for us to be wise guides for you and your teams, we must first do the work in our own selves. This has been our commitment from the beginning of our coaching practice and will continue to be paramount in the years to come.

And what seems so powerful about that for us is that we can see, name, and celebrate the ways that this work has contributed to real and lasting transformation in our lives! Are we done? No, not by a long shot. After seeing the transformation this work has resulted in, do we want more? Yes! Once we saw the fruits of a truly new way of being and showing up, day by day, month by month, year by year, those old ways of being that led to feelings of being exhausted, frustrated, and overwhelmed just grew less and less desirable.

I get it, you might be reading this thinking, "Yes, let's go!" Or perhaps you've read that and thought, "OK, great, but you don't know what my life is like." If you're the "let's go!" kind of person, pump the brakes a little bit. If you're the latter, to you, I say, "You're right; I don't know what your life is like." Our lives and life experiences are as diverse as the quality of hot dogs at baseball stadiums (that's really diverse, in case you didn't know!).

Either way, we (both Chris and Kurt) see tremendous value in sharing with you a bit of our own transformational journeys. Not to pat ourselves on the backs. Not to give you a template to apply in your own lives. Rather, we share these following stories humbly, hoping that we might build trust with you, the reader, that you might see that we are willing to walk the walk with you. But it's also to share with you something we hold so dear: the idea that what has always been in our lives need not stay the same going forward, and we get to be active participants in making that happen.

All this, dear reader, is for the sake of your own flourishing. There is no doubt that leading and living in the twenty-first century requires a lot from you. If you are exhausted, frustrated, and overloaded with any or all of it, this book, from front to back, is designed to help you move in the direction of contentment, fulfillment, and wholeness—whatever that looks like for you.

Hear us say to you one more time: You don't have to go through life simply surviving anymore. You don't have to keep regretting the way you show up in meetings. You don't have to keep losing your temper over and over again, unsure of why it happens. You are not made to merely survive; you are made to thrive! Transformation is possible and available to you, even today.

We invite you to settle in, feel the ground beneath your feet, and take a few deep breaths. Inhale for four seconds, hold that breath for seven seconds, and exhale it for eight seconds. Repeat three or four times.

Welcome! You're in the right place. The transformational journey begins here.

CHAPTER 1

# THE TRANSFORMATIONAL JOURNEY

*You can't get rid of any part, so the best you can do is to help it transform.*
—JAY EARLY

My journey (Kurt) began a long time ago, nearly a decade ago, as I write this. To give you the clearest picture of how my story starts, we have to go to a long table (more like three average tables combined) of seminarians having some good food and even better drinks at New Holland Brewery in Holland, Michigan. It's there at that table that I have my earliest memory of Chris (yes, the same Chris I'm coauthoring this book with), inviting me into a formational journey with him. This was a journey that included much self-discovery and one that would hopefully lead to a more whole version of each participant.

Chris shared with me and a couple of other peers the value that this process had provided him. I don't remember specifics, but I remember that Chris was adamant that the process was not only a gift to participate in but that some sort of process of formation and transformation like this should be required of leaders at all levels.

So the invite came: "Kurt, do you want to join me?" And in response to that invitation, I did what any of us might do . . . I said, "Psshh, nah, I'm good. I don't really need that sort of process." Internally, I went a little further than what I voiced to Chris in the moment. What I really thought was, "No way, I'm totally fine—I just need to learn more tactical leadership things, and I'll be fine!" I could not have been more misguided.

Eventually, though, I began to see the fruit of this process in Chris's life as we navigated a pretty demanding season of life together. I heard Chris use language like, "I wonder what that's about," and, "Let's get curious about that." At some point, I decided to join Chris in the formation process he'd shared with us at New Holland Brewery, and the rest, as they say, is history.

After some reluctance and maybe a dose of skepticism, I dove into the process of self-discovery with some really kind help from a few people much further in their own journeys. I started to realize that even I, the guy who said, "Nah, I'm good," had been impacted by experiences in my past. No matter how much I didn't want to admit it, it was just true—neither good nor bad, just true. I began to see that those experiences really drove the bus, so to speak, of how I showed up in my work, in my life at home with my family, and in the ways I'd play in my downtime.

For a minute (as my teenager might say), this was largely theory for me. I could see how these things were impacting my life, but they hadn't impacted me to the point that I needed to get serious about addressing them for real by getting into action.

That was the case until my second year of seminary and my first year as a full-time staff member in a local church. That's when the journey and the tools I was learning started to get really real. They became much more important and, dare I say, necessary for my well-being. I simply could not continue living the way I was living without a significant impact on me, my family, and those I was trying to lead.

Up to that point, I'd always felt out of place at seminary. I was a nontraditional student, and I'd never studied or written anything at that educational level. I felt like a fish out of water. Tangibly, it really did feel like everyone was looking at me, judging me every step of the way. Peers, faculty, professors, you name it—I truly believed I was one bad paper away from being found out as an imposter. It's not an exaggeration to say that every time I hovered my mouse over the "SUBMIT" button to turn in an assignment, the wave of fear that said, "This is the one," would sweep over me as real a feeling as a spring wind in northwest Iowa (It's windy, trust me).

At the same time, something else was happening in me. I was settling into my new staff position, part of which included participating in board meetings with other senior staff and volunteer leaders. I noticed that I was not showing up in those spaces like I wanted to. Or maybe more accurately said, I would sit in those meetings trying to calculate what I was going to say, just waiting for the chance to say it, often missing the majority of the meeting's purpose itself while doing those calculations.

Not only that, but I would predictably almost always leave those meetings telling myself one of two stories, either, "You dummy, why did you say that thing you said?" or "See, I told you that you wouldn't say that thing you wanted to say." I'd either overshare or under-share. Neither felt authentic. And none of this—the way I showed up in my job and the way I showed up in my schoolwork—was sustainable. White-knuckling my life like that was literally draining the life out of me.

What I know now, and what I learned then, is that it felt inauthentic because it was indeed inauthentic. The Kurt that showed up in those ways was the false Kurt, not the truest form of Kurt. It was the Kurt who saw nearly every part of the world as unsafe. The Kurt who could never get to the top of the hamster wheel of safety.

I can look back now and see that all of this behavior and all of those patterns could be traced back to a *protective promise* I made to myself in middle school—a promise made in our first formations to stay safe and get the attention and affection we want and need. It went all the way back to someone important in my life (a super well-meaning and loving person who cared for me deeply) saying to me, "Imagine how good you'd be if you tried more."

Devastated . . . thanks for asking. Subconsciously, I promised myself I would never again let someone see me as incompetent because being seen as incompetent equaled danger to middle school Kurt's nervous system. So all those years later, in a boardroom or on an online class submission page, the threat and danger associated with looking incompetent felt so real, leading me to do all sorts of things to avoid it—even things I'm not proud of today.

It's not a stretch to say that the things I learned about myself that season literally changed my life. That season, as hard as the work was that it required, was the beginning part of the journey in which I grasped agency in deciding how I wanted to be in all areas of my life. From there, I continued to engage in the formation process Chris invited me to, to the point of completing that journey and facilitating that process for others.

I began working with a coach of my own, who would continually (and gently) hold up a mirror in front of me, allowing me to see what was so in me. I find it hard to find the words to convey my gratitude for Chris, those other coaches, and a handful of other "wise guides" who have helped me do the hard work of self-discovery and taking responsibility for my own growth—the growth that Chris and I humbly invite you into in this book.

And what's also true is that the need for me to do the work continues. It does not stop. I continue to use these same tools and practices we offer you to learn more about myself and to practice and try on new ways of being that hopefully work better and more sustainably than the old ways.

I named one protective promise for you—that I would never again let someone see me as incompetent. I've worked through many more, some of which will be shared later in the book, but I uncovered a new protective promise just recently. And by recently, I mean a mere matter of months before writing this. I celebrate the tools and the thought processes to navigate that well. The work continues.

From that initial season of growth on, I developed a passion for this work, not only using these tools and practices in my own life but also helping others do the same. As I continued to do the work, I was fortunate enough to have the chance to facilitate this work with others long before launching the Brimstone Coaching Group in 2024. Frankly, this work has become my heartbeat and my passion. It's become the thing that I will devote my life to doing. It's the thing that undergirds and props up any form of leadership I find myself in.

I am different, and I want you to be different. I am a more true version of me today, and I want you to be the most true version of you today too!

---

It's not easy for me (Chris) to talk about when this work really began for me. The truth is, it began for me during a painful season of life when I needed to become curious about who I was, why I did the things I did, and what transformation might look like.

Much of the early work of beginning to understand how I had gotten to the place I found myself in was completed on my own. In silence and reflection. Time spent driving down the road with the sound off, wondering why I showed up in the world the way I did. The early journey was aided by my pastor, a therapist, and my wife. They patiently walked with me as I turned inward so that the outward expression of the person people experienced could move toward the truest version of the person I was created to be.

Truth be told, I was unpleasant to be around a lot of the time. I often left games my kids played in exhausted, frustrated, and overwhelmed with shame and guilt at how I had behaved. It wasn't fun to sit near me either. To anyone and everyone who experienced me in those ways, I would love to hear the impact I had on you for the sake of cleaning up the messes I made.

Honestly, I approached more than one referee on a Friday night, apologizing for how I had shown up at the game on Tuesday night. Then, two bad calls into the game, there I would go again. More than one person asked the question, "Why can't you just sit there? Why do you have to behave that way?"

We introduced you to the idea of protective promises in the Introduction, and Kurt mentioned one that he made in his story above. When we didn't feel safe at some point earlier in our childhood, we made an unconscious promise to ourselves to avoid the pain of the past. At the time, the promise may have been helpful, but in adulthood, it has likely outlived its useful life.

My journey of self-discovery highlighted three seasons of my life. The earliest protective promise I made took root as a six-year-old. A series of experiences caused me to believe that I was nothing but a naughty little boy, and the greatest fear I had was that another person would think or find out just how bad I was. The protective promise I made was along these lines: "I perform to seek approval."

The other two experiences happened roughly four months apart as a fourteen-year-old. The first is hard to explain unless you have some theological background, but here goes. I had completed all the classes required by the local church we attended to be "confirmed." Confirmation Sunday included the class standing in front of the church, professing what we believed, and then receiving our first Communion. When my family and I went forward to take Communion, I was skipped.

In theological circles, when I have shared this story, audible gasps always follow those three words: "I was skipped." In that moment, everything I believed about myself was confirmed, and it had a negative impact on my behavior for years to come. Again, the protective promise was unconscious, and I will say more about that in a paragraph or two.

The second experience happened that summer. I went away for a week to participate in a basketball camp at a local college. It had been a good week, and I returned home in time for the county fair. Country singer Steve Wariner (any of you ever heard of him?) was going to perform, and I was supposed to see the girl I was dating at that concert. This is pre-cell phones, pre-SnapChat, pre virtually everything in the early eighties, and she completely ghosted me.

I was devastated and had no way of processing the pain. The protective promise I made because of that experience was short and sweet: "I will not be controlled."

Typing these paragraphs brings back some of those teenage feelings. My neck stiffens, a pit forms in my gut, and I feel a little bit helpless. The autonomic nervous system stores these experiences, and without the work of self-discovery, I might just go off and do what I do when I feel those feelings.

Every person has an autonomic nervous system. It's a network of nerves that controls the automatic function of the human body needed for survival—usually, things we don't think about, like breathing. The autonomic nervous system is the part that connects our brain to most of our internal organs.

What I want you to grasp is those two experiences as a fourteen-year-old do not have to repeat themselves. But when I see injustice in the world—which both experiences felt like at the time—those feelings come rushing back, and, unprocessed, the things I do to not be controlled by my feelings or another person kick in. Those things I do in this state are never helpful.

Now closer to sixty than fifty, I know that it was a human mistake at the altar that Confirmation Sunday. It was not malice, nor did God actually think the things I believed about myself. Those ways are not the ways God looks at me or any of creation.

I can rationalize these experiences now and make sense of them. In this moment, I can get into the balcony, as Kurt and I like to say, and see the experiences for what they were. I can say, "It's okay; I'm okay," and have it actually be true. However, there are times that I am blindsided by a situation; those feelings associated with the protective promise trigger something in me, and I lose the experience of safety that we, as human beings, so desperately long for.

Not feeling safe and trying to climb back to the top of the hamster wheel, I move toward some people, I move against others, and sometimes I move away from people. If I move toward you, I try to win your approval or make sure you think well of me. If I move against you, I can demonize or villainize you. I argue and fight to convince you that I am right. And if I move away, I distance at best and totally cut off at worst.

---

Behaving in these ways is not unique to Kurt or to me. You do some version of these things too. Like Kurt, I have had some "wise guides" throughout my journey, and I am grateful for their compassion, empathy, and patience with me in this transformational journey.

Like Kurt, dear reader, I've given my life to this work. The desire of my heart is to help you understand why you do what you do when you do what you do. If you are exhausted, frustrated, and overloaded with the way things are, I promise you that contentment, fulfillment, and wholeness are available to you.

How do I know? I've seen it in Kurt, and I've experienced it myself. I can't wait to share more with you about the journey so that you can share in this transformational work.

CHAPTER

## 2

# WHY DO WE DO THIS WORK?

*Truly, the best thing any of us have to bring to leadership is our own transforming selves.*
—RUTH HALEY BARTON

We were meant to work one job—not two! We know what you're thinking: "But Kurt and Chris, I don't work two jobs." Or maybe you're thinking, "You're right—I actually work three jobs to support my family."

We understand that could be true too. Maybe a more accurate way to say that statement is we believe that each of us goes through our days and our workdays doing this invisible but heavy "second" job. Not only are we not compensated for this extra job, but we don't receive any benefit from it either. Whether the first job is a paid gig or raising a family outside a traditional employment structure, we'd say that this second job actually makes doing that first job much harder and our efforts less effective.

Maybe you've heard of Robert Kegan, a developmental psychologist who spent forty years at the Harvard Graduate School of Education. To paraphrase Kegan, the assertion is that this second job is the job of hiding or "faking it till you make it." Or maybe you work really hard to make sure your cubicle mate doesn't think you're lazy.

Stop here and imagine just for a second whether or not you have a second job like that.

## IT'S TIME TO QUIT YOUR SECOND JOB

I (Kurt) had a second job that demanded much of me for a long time, even though I had no idea I was doing it! Remember that protective promise I mentioned in the last chapter? The one that said, "I will never let anyone see me as incompetent"? That turned into a second job in a really visible and detrimental way.

> "I will never let anyone see me as incompetent."
> —Kurt Bush

I was in a leadership position within a multi-campus church, and once a week, I'd find myself around a conference table with other leaders, as well as other scholarly and academic-type people. Honestly, these people were brilliant. I can look back now and see the gift it was to be at the table with them.

But it didn't feel like a gift at the time! Maybe you see the problem coming into focus. It took very little to kick my autonomic nervous system into high gear, which would begin the process of saying, "DANGER!! These people are going to think you're dumb if you speak up!" I wanted to, but I rarely could muster the courage to do so. OR, if I did speak up, it was after MUCH internal deliberation and calculation.

We refer to that as my second job because it took my focus away from what I was actually supposed to be doing in that meeting. And maybe you've already caught this, too, that the reality was the second job didn't take away the responsibilities of my first job. So I'd leave that conference room table with no less responsibility for the tasks that I was supposed to be using that collaborative time to work on. It was exhausting for me and was detrimental to the effectiveness of my first job.

Reading that story brings back some memories for me (Chris). I remember serving on a board with a variety of other leaders. The people I served on this board with were of varied ages and professional backgrounds. I was early in my leadership journey and still trying to find my voice. The thing most true about this time in my life is that it predated virtually all of my self-awareness and self-discovery work.

One of the other leaders on the board was twenty-five years my senior. He led a major nonprofit and had served on this board a number of times throughout the years. He was measured in his responses, and when voices began to elevate in a meeting, his would decrease. It was a creative tactic, really.

I showed up to these meetings prepared and did my best to "play full out," to be as fully me as I could be in every meeting. That was my job in this role as a board member. The second job I often found myself working in this role, however, was to do whatever it took for the other board members to not think (or find out) that I was worthless.

The problem is that I didn't know what I didn't know about that. The aforementioned leader and I were often at odds. He was really conservative in the way he made decisions, while I was willing to take risks. He was more measured in his responses while I said what I was thinking. And the way I felt after each and every meeting was exhausted, frustrated, and overwhelmed.

I rarely felt safe in those meetings. It was more than enough to handle my responsibilities as a board member, but being triggered often resulted in the cover of my second job being blown.

It has been said that systems often get exactly what they were designed to get. That was the case with this board and the relationship between this older leader and me until I became aware of the second job I was trying to work and the negative impact it had on me and my leadership.

Remember the friends we introduced you to a little bit ago? They all have second jobs too. Whether aware of it or not, they were doing things that kept them from their first "job" of being fully who they are.

- Bruce's second job was the job of constantly proving to himself and others that he matters.
- Elizabeth worked a second job in the gym, fulfilling the unwritten commitment to success at all costs.
- Kevin found himself giving all of who he was, all his energy, to the job that nobody actually asked him to do: to protect everyone.
- Lucy clocked in each day to measure up to the standards of her parents, though they were no longer around to check her work.

You get the picture. These second jobs consume at every turn.

## YOUR SUCCESS IN LEADERSHIP HINGES ON YOUR PERSONAL GROWTH

In their book *An Everyone Culture*, Robert Kegan and Lisa Laskow Lahey introduce the concept of organizations being deliberately developmental. The idea is that companies and organizations devoted to the development of their employees as whole selves, over and against viewing people as brains on a stick who do a thing, are far more successful.[1]

In deliberately developmental systems, people are more free to be themselves and not continue working that exhausting, frustrating, and overwhelming second job. They become more successful individually, the teams and companies they lead are more successful corporately, and life itself is more enjoyable as a whole.

This is why I (Kurt) think we'd be remiss if we didn't also take the

---

[1] Robert Keegan and Lisa Laskow Lahey, *An Everyone Culture: Becoming a Deliberately Developmental Organization* (Boston, MA: Harvard Business School Publishing, 2016).

opportunity to speak to those of you who have employees or teams that you're responsible for leading. What sorts of second jobs do you think your team members are doing today? How might your team's first job be affected by those second jobs? And can you imagine the potential your teams hold if each member was able to do the work to set that second job aside?

_____

_____

_____

_____

_____

_____

Let us say again: We are meant to work one job, not two! You don't have to do that second job any longer.

One reason we believe this is true is that an increasing number of employers actually care about the development of their employees in twenty-first-century North America. According to the LinkedIn Workplace Learning Report (2024), 47 percent of all employers are offering employees some form of mentoring or coaching.[2] The tide has begun to turn, one reason being that leaders themselves are becoming increasingly emotionally mature. Thankfully, it seems the days of "come to work, do a task, receive money in return" are coming to an end. Emotional intelligence (defined as the ability to understand and manage your emotions, as well as recognize the emotions of those around you) has brought with it a heightened sense of the value of other human beings. Employers who lead successful

---

[2] "Workforce Learning Report 2024," LinkedIn Learning, https://learning.linkedin.com/resources/workplace-learning-report-2024.

companies as we move deeper into the twenty-first century will be people who continue to grow in their own leadership.

In her book *Strengthening the Soul of Your Leadership*, Ruth Haley Barton posits the idea that leaders who are not growing in their own leadership are basically disqualified from leading others.[3] We couldn't agree more!

Think about it. Remember Jack, the young marketing team lead from the Introduction? Jack was good at his job, like really good at it. But because he was dealing with his own protective promise and was limited in his productivity by having to work the second job of not allowing anyone else to know about his struggles, his team plateaued. And so did Jack's career—until he got a new boss. This new boss was interested in Jack and who he was. As his boss, this woman was not threatened by who Jack was and the skill he had. In fact, because she was continuing to grow in her own leadership, she encouraged Jack to connect with a coach who could help him along his own self-discovery journey.

If the new boss had not come along, Jack may still be toiling away, working both jobs and not enjoying life. But because she did, and because she continued to understand herself in deepening ways, she could encourage his growth and success rather than be threatened by it. She also knew that her organization *needed* a whole, more authentic version of Jack showing up at work.

## YOU DON'T HAVE TO WHITE-KNUCKLE YOUR WAY THROUGH LIFE

Lastly, we want to say it is important to engage in the transformational journey because there is more to adulting than merely white-knuckling your way through life.

---

[3] Ruth Haley Barton, *Strengthening the Soul of Your Leadership: Seeking God in the Crucible of Ministry* (Illinois: InterVaristy Press, 2018).

If you drive in the city or live in a part of the country that requires you to drive in blizzard conditions, you know what the phrase white-knuckling means. White-knuckling is the term used to describe a process of fighting or powering through a situation that you find extremely anxiety-producing. Kurt often says that he used to just think this was what it meant to live.

I (Kurt) know a thing or two about literal white-knuckling. There was a season in my life when riding my mountain bike was a huge part of my life. Multiple times a week, I could be found on a single-track trail in the woods in the bluffy area along the Mississippi River.

Anyone who rides a bike regularly knows about Strava. For those of you who don't, Strava is an app that will use the location services on your phone to keep track of your rides and all the data from each ride, like elevation change, total distance, and total time. But it also does one more really important thing—it keeps track of who is fastest on any given trail among all Strava users. (Chris says he has a love/hate relationship with Strava!)

In the summer of 2019, I decided I was going to be the fastest rider on a trail called Kickapoo Down. It was an extremely fast and gnarly (that's mountain bike slang, trust me) downhill trail that was all of thirty seconds long. I knew my goal: be the fastest to ever log a time on Kickapoo Down.

I'd pull up to the park with my bike and just ride this one short trail over and over and over again. And by about the fifth time down, I'd be exhausted. My arms would be completely out of gas, and nearing the end of the season, I was nowhere near the KOM (king of the mountain). Why? Because I was literally white-knuckling my bike down the hill. It depleted me physically, and I was SLOW!

In search of speed, I found a resource that taught me to grip loosely and to stop white-knuckling the handlebars. It worked! I stopped forcing the bike where I wanted it to go, and I let it do what it does. I stayed looser and could ride longer. Now, I didn't get KOM, but I did finally get top ten (18 of 1,330 today) speed on Kickapoo Down.

I get it—it's not a perfect analogy, but I do think it's a good analogy. For so long, I white-knuckled my way through my life, and I wonder if you feel the same. Often, I'd feel out of control, way behind, or unsuccessful (insert your own thing here), so I'd metaphorically hold on even tighter. I'd try harder, I'd push more, and I'd sacrifice more. And none of that would get the results I thought it should get.

Or maybe for you, it feels like you're constantly behind, trying to catch up. Or you're constantly one mistake away from being discovered as an imposter. Those things also make you "grab harder" and white-knuckle even more. And like white-knuckling on my mountain bike, that sort of white-knuckling your way through life is just not sustainable.

You just can't do it. Dare I say: We are not made for white-knuckling. Instead of producing results or helping us get ahead, it will only lead to fatigue and potentially all the way to burnout.

I was well into my thirties before someone told me, "You don't have to white-knuckle through life anymore!" So allow us explicitly to say it to you: Reader, you don't have to white-knuckle through life anymore! You need not feel exhausted, frustrated, or overloaded any longer!

Part of the trouble is that when you're white-knuckling your way through life, it's easy to assume that everyone is and that this white-knuckling experience is really what it means to be an adult in this time we live in. And while it might be true that everyone around you is white-knuckling their way through life, believe me, white-knuckling is NOT really what it means to be an adult. There are other, more whole ways to adult (yes, I used "adult" in verb form).

Now, we want to be really clear: Letting go of our tendency to white-knuckle is hard work. It's often work we don't know how to do, which is why it's so important to begin the transformational journey with a wise guide.

Much like a real physical journey, the transformational journey requires some things from you. We invite you on this journey toward wholeness with us, and we invite you to bring a few things with you. Namely, you'll need to bring *grit*, a healthy dose of *courage*, and all the *honesty* you've got.

## WHAT TO PACK FOR THE TRANSFORMATIONAL JOURNEY

*Grit.* Who uses that word today anyway? It's certainly not a word that we hear daily, but it's absolutely necessary for the transformational journey!

What is grit, you may ask? In the Oxford Dictionary, "grit" (as used in this context) is defined as "resolve; strength of character." What I hear in that definition is a willingness to keep going on the journey, even when it gets really tough. And it will.

The reality is that many of us have white-knuckled and lived in our old patterns of behavior for decades. So when we try on something new and different from what we've always done, the temptation to abandon that new way of being can be really strong.

When I (Kurt) go to a restaurant, I typically get some variation of the food I know I'll like. It's known. I'm not going to spend money on something I might not like. I don't like to risk making that meal a disappointment. While I know I will like what I've ordered, there's a very good chance I'm missing the most delicious item on the menu for the sake of the food I know.

Living our lives in old ways of being is similar. I know what those old ways require of me. I know the workarounds of those old ways really well because I made them over the course of time. New ways of being, however, while they may be extremely freeing and life-changing, they're still new and untested. What if I don't like them? What if they're much harder to live into?

Wholeness is ALWAYS better than hiding and always better than white-knuckling. But the temptation to bail out and go back to the old, known ways will be strong along the way. Get that grit packed up and ready to go!

*Courage* is necessary for the journey as well. The definition of the word courage that I (Chris) appreciate the most is this one: strength in the face of pain or grief.

Let's face it: Anyone can be brave when assured of a positive outcome. If you are a runner and the 400m is your specialty, there isn't much at stake challenging the average human to a race when you can fly around the track in less than forty-nine seconds. Maybe you are a trained vocalist, and one night, while out with your friends, the local watering hole has a karaoke competition. There isn't much need for courage for you, is there?

Kurt and I are both baseball lovers, so this may only grab his attention, but here goes. When I made the decision to go back to school to get a master's degree, it required all the courage I could muster. I'd always joked with people that I graduated college, got a job based on my abilities, and eventually built my own little business empire—and all the while, nobody had ever asked for my college transcripts.

I completed the application on time, reached out to the college where I had done my undergrad work for copies of my transcript, and wrote a letter of apology to the school I was seeking acceptance to because my collegiate GPA was barely above the Mendoza Line (go ahead, give that a quick Google search).

This is why it took all the courage I could muster to apply for graduate school. I promised myself early in my childhood that no one would ever think or find out that I was a failure! Now, academics with as many consonants behind their names as there are in the English alphabet would have the proof I feared.

I'll never forget the day the director of admissions from Western Theological Seminary called me. "Would you like the good news or the bad news?" he asked. He proceeded to tell me I had been accepted, but I would be on academic probation. I laughed out loud, almost uncontrollably, and responded: "Hey, it's a miracle that God could or would ever love me. I'm not worried about being on probation."

All of that is true, and every time I wrote a post for a discussion board, had to turn in an assignment, or showed up for intensive weeks on campus, courage would have to be exercised. I white-knuckled my way through seminary as I was introduced to the concepts in this book alongside my master's program. Honestly, at the moment, I'm not sure which learning is more significant.

My academic struggles started early, back as that six-year-old version of myself who needed to protect himself at all costs. I did not know why I never tried academically because I didn't understand the pain or grief of those early years.

Reader, we want you to pack courage for the journey, as well. We are honored to be your wise guides in exercising the strength you need to face the pain or grief you may have experienced.

The last thing to pack is maybe the hardest part of all of this: *honesty*.

Maybe you've heard the following sentiment, often associated with the fear toddlers might feel at bedtime. "If I don't look under the bed, then there is no monster under the bed." Well, monsters don't work that way. And neither does the journey of transformation and the requisite work of self-discovery.

We're inviting you to be honest with yourself. Be honest about what is true in your life today. Be honest with yourself about the parts of you and your life that you wish were different, and maybe even the parts you don't believe can EVER ACTUALLY be different. Be honest with yourself in saying that there might be times when your behavior or patterns of living don't align with how you'd prefer to live. Be honest with yourself that, indeed, those things CAN change.

For me (Kurt), there has been little harder in my own journey than having to be honest that I don't have my life all figured out. But transformation began with that one step of honesty, recognizing I was simply surviving with the whitest knuckles I'd ever seen.

We're inviting you to be honest with others as well. As we've said already, we don't journey alone. Part of the immense value of that wise guide is their ability to hold up a mirror for you so you might see parts of yourself you otherwise can't.

I love a trip to the barber. Shout out, Kapper! I have a standing barber appointment every other Friday. Without fail, every appointment ends with Daimon handing me a literal mirror and spinning me around in the chair so I can see all parts of my head and his handiwork that I just cannot see otherwise.

Once our wise guides hold that mirror up, we have the chance to decide what we want to do with what we're seeing. Often, that includes conversations and interactions with others in our lives who will play a role in our transformation.

It feels appropriate to clarify: Be as honest as you can be right now. To Kurt's point, being able to acknowledge that we don't have it all figured out is one of the prime places to foster transformation.

The reality is we all know some things about ourselves. We know our names, what foods we like to eat, what movies we like to watch, and things like that. There are also things we don't know. Some of us might not know that we aren't good at bowling (I'm not sharing that story right now); some of us aren't aware that we are carrying the smell of the hog buildings with us wherever we go (the risk of living in agricultural places); and others are unaware that the mint from that mojito is in their teeth. For most of us, the things we don't know outweigh the things we do know.

Far greater still, however, is the rather massive part of ourselves where we don't know what we don't know.

Ignorance is bliss, they say. Until it isn't. The things we don't know that we don't know result in us white-knuckling our way through life. This is why it's important to engage in the transformational journey. It's why you need to pack grit, courage, and honesty.

Reader, we dare you to be honest.

CHAPTER

# 3

# THE TRANSFORMATIONAL EQUATION

*The thrill of life is not about who we are, but about who we are in the process of becoming."*
—DAVID EAGLEMAN,
AUTHOR OF *LIVEWIRED*

In order to loosen our grip on the handlebars so we can give our knuckles a break, we've asked you to pack grit, courage, and honesty for the journey. We also want to provide you with some assistance, as this journey will also require both your brains and a *Transformational Equation* (**E**ncounter + **R**eflection = **T**ransformation) to lead you.

American psychologist William James once coined the term "plasticity." James understood that plastic objects are able to be molded and shaped and then hold that shape. James's contention was that the brain had similar capabilities.

In his book *Livewired*, renowned neurosurgeon David Eagleman talks about the idea of neuroplasticity. "So it is with the brain: experience changes it, and it retains the change."[4] The human brain may have taken

---

[4] David Eagleman, *Livewired: The Inside Story of the Ever-Changing Brain* (New York: Doubleday, 2020), 13–14.

in information early in our lives that led to us behaving in particular ways. The good news for you—and for Kurt and I—is that the brain may also take in new information that results in behavior change. And as it experiences the change, the brain retains the change.

This is mind-blowing for many of us. And, for those who know us best, it is also likely confusing that we would reference science—let alone neuroscience—and math. To you, friends, we say this is the power of transformation! (Thanks, Rodger, for opening my eyes to quantum physics, and Cory Brandt, can you believe I'm referencing science?)

As we've engaged in the transformational journey, however, we see the relevance of math and science. We are not the same people today as we were last year, and we won't be the same next year as we are today. Eagleman explains that the circuitry of the brain is full of life, and the connections between neurons blossom, die, and reconfigure all the time.

We see a similar transformation when we explore metamorphosis, the process a caterpillar goes through en route to becoming a butterfly.

This is where we derived the name of our coaching practice, The Brimstone Coaching Group. The brimstone is the butterfly with the longest life span on the butterfly side of its life, and the transformational process it engages leads to the longest life.

You are being invited into a transformational journey as well. The word *metamorphoo* is a Greek word defined as "the process of transformation from an immature form to an adult form in two more distinct stages." To be clear, you are not being called immature, nor are we calling you infants. You are who you are today, and you are more than good enough to journey with us. Both things are true.

Here's one way we think about maturity, growth, and progress. If you have kids or helped raise kids, you know that, really, the ultimate goal of that work is to form and shape a fully functioning adult. It's widely thought (at least in the midwestern American context we're writing in) that a child becomes a potentially fully functioning adult at the age of eighteen. But before you can become a fully functioning adult, you have to celebrate a seventh birthday.

Seventh birthdays are weird, aren't they? There's really no milestone at seven. Seventh birthday parties are weird for kids too. Some kids act closer to ten years old, while others go the other way and still act like they are five years old. And they're all loud! The point is although we really want these kids of ours to be a fully functioning eighteen-year-old, that doesn't take away the importance of turning seven. Obviously, there's no child in history that could turn eighteen without first turning seven . . . then eight . . . you get the picture. We'd also never hold it against our seven-year-old kids. No, we celebrate the turning over of another year.

The same is true in this metaphor. We might be infants in our emotional maturity and self-awareness today, and that's OK because we can't be fully mature without first turning seven. And we'll celebrate every seemingly mundane milestone of growth along the way! As leaders, we believe that the kind of growth and increased maturity that lead us to become whole adults is available to every human being, including you.

A guy named Paul once said it this way: "Do not conform to the pattern of this world, but be transformed by the renewing of your mind. Then you will be able to test and approve what God's will is—his good, pleasing and perfect will" (Romans 12:2).

As we read those words, we feel clear that there is a level of intentionality that a person must embrace to experience transformation. Our lived experience tells us at Brimstone Coaching Group that the journey toward maturity and transformation is one that is slow and happens over time. It's a LONG journey. In a world that is quick to label slow processes as "failures" or "ineffective," hear us say again that transformation *is* possible, and we are here to assist you in this process.

## RENEWING YOUR MIND

The adaptive challenge before you is an invitation designed with renewing of your mind at heart. Ronald Heifetz and Marty Linsky describe the adaptive learning process as one that requires observation, interpretation, and intervention.⁵ We like this idea and have put our own twist on it.

We follow the process of metamorphosis in a way, but the point is to help you move from the immature form of yourself into a fully formed adult. You were created on purpose for a purpose, and our goal is to help you overcome your protective promises (discussed in Chapters 1 and 2) by replacing them with purposeful ones as you read on.

> *"The brain chronically adjusts itself to reflect its challenges and goals. It molds its resources to match the requirements of its circumstances. When it doesn't possess what it needs, it sculpts it."⁶*

I (Chris) love this idea, and I am keenly aware of just how little time I used to give myself—and my brain—to adjust. I had deadlines to meet, goals to attain, and revenue to generate, all for the sake of meeting a need I didn't know I had. I'm not sure my brain had the time to even realize what it didn't possess. Racing from one thing to the next, the pace was frenetic. When I look back on those early years of adulting, it simply makes me exhausted. The eighty- and ninety-hour weeks in pursuit of the almighty dollar left no time to process anything that was happening around me.

Research has shown that people who engage more in self-reflection have better cognition and improved glucose metabolism, as shown by brain imaging.⁷ This is good news for us and impacts the way we consider the transformational journey.

We are not only convinced by math and science—philosophy has some

---

⁵ Ronald Abadian Heifetz, Alexander Grashow, and Martin Linsky, *The Practice of Adaptive Leadership: Tools and Tactics for Chang in Your Organization* (Boston, MA: Harvard Business Press, 2009).

⁶ Eagleman, *Livewired*, 12.

⁷ Harriet Demnitz-King, MSc, Julie Gonneaud, PhD, et al, "Association of Self-Reflection with Cognition and Brain Health in Cognitively Unimpaired Older Adults," *Neurology* 99 (no. 13): 1422-1431, September 27, 2022, https://www.neurology.org/doi/10.1212/WNL.0000000000200951.

influence as well. It was Socrates who was credited with the saying, "The unexamined life is not worth living." As people living 2500 years after the death of Socrates, we affirm his beliefs!

*The Brimstone Transformational Equation*
$$E + R = T$$
*Encounter + Reflection = Transformation*

Our experience with this equation has proven to be true, and we've seen hundreds of lives changed by understanding encounters and reflecting on their significance for transformation. First, let's go deeper into the idea of harnessing the power of daily encounters.

We've seen this equation prove its power in the lives of hundreds of people. But first, we saw it to be true in our lives. What's true for both of us is that there was a time when we were unable to even see the encounters we had on a daily basis, much less reflect on them. But as we look back, we can see the real value in recognizing and reflecting as close to real time as possible!

I (Kurt) used to call Chris from a place of frustration, "venting," as they say, about the people I was called to lead. "They aren't doing this" or "they aren't doing that." I was literally just complaining in real time. And I'll never forget what Chris would do because it truly was the beginning of seeing the importance of this equation as it pertains to the transformation of my leadership.

Chris would listen well, letting me say what was on my mind. Then, gently and kindly, he would ask, "What part are you playing in this situation?" The first couple times he startled me with this question, my answer was, "Nothing—didn't you hear what I just said?" But slowly, I saw the real gift that question held. It invited me to recognize that an encounter had happened and walked me graciously into reflection of it! It's out of many situations just like this one that the Transformational Equation was birthed.

## RECOGNIZING YOUR ENCOUNTERS

Life in the twenty-first century moves close to the speed of light, and our work/life balance feels like walking between two high-rise buildings on nothing more than a fishing line. Our faith in that fishing line and in our own ability to maintain any sort of balance as we walk from work to life and back again sometimes reveals ridiculous confidence and bravado. More often, it reveals our paralysis and lack of awareness.

We do the same things over and over and over again, expecting different results. There is a word for this kind of behavior—we believe you know what that word is—and we want you to know that it doesn't have to be this way.

> What if you could achieve work/life balance?
> What if you didn't have to do the same thing over and over again?
> What if you could experience transformation?

At Brimstone Coaching Group, we believe that every human being has hundreds, if not thousands, of encounters every day. An encounter is defined as an unexpected or casual meeting with someone or something. We don't mean to conflate the word encounter with scheduled conferences, experiences, or meetings. There is something profound about the unexpected or casual nature of encounters that impact us. In contrast with the scheduled "encounters," it's often the unscheduled and unplanned nature of the majority of our encounters that make them so impactful. In fact, we might have multiple encounters in the course of a meeting.

Bear with us for just a moment. In a meeting with the CEO of your company, you may have an encounter with her as you enter the room. A snide comment aimed in your direction may be one encounter you have. When your boss makes a derogatory comment about you in front of her, that is another encounter.

Or maybe an encounter looks like that moment when you miss the stoplight changing to green by one-tenth of a second, and the person behind you hits their horn, prodding you to get moving. Or when the barista at that new coffee shop you're trying for the first time calls out "Americano for Kayla" when really your name is Kyla.

Or maybe it's when you open social media to see "that other parent" who's posted pictures of the way she cut her kids' lunch sandwiches into dinosaur shapes while you're just trying not to forget your kid needs a lunch (that definitely wasn't a real story from Kurt's life—OK, it definitely was a real story).

We think you get it. These are all encounters that we can so easily gloss right over every single day.

One researcher showed the average adult has anywhere from 7,000–15,000 encounters with other people during the course of the day. Additionally, I (Chris) can say that I have hundreds of other "encounters" each day as I scroll through social media for news and entertainment purposes. These encounters, each one of them, have an impact on me, my life, and my work. I said things like:

"I am exhausted."
"I am at the end of my rope."
"I just can't take it anymore."
"It never seems to end."

These are just a few of the phrases I have used to express my own exhaustion, frustration, and overwhelm. I imagine many of you, if not all of you, can relate. And while recognizing our encounters is important, there's still more to do with them. How do those encounters lead to transformation? Through *reflection*.

## REFLECTING ON YOUR ENCOUNTERS

As I'm writing this chapter, I (Kurt) experienced a real-time encounter. I'm teaching a college class for the first time at a private college in the town where I live. I've never done this sort of teaching before, but I've always wanted to have the opportunity to try it. Just a week ago, about halfway through the course, I had a student reach out to ask a very specific question about a part of the class she was struggling with.

Every week, in this fully online course, there are two quizzes for the students to complete from the week's reading and lectures. Those quizzes are open-note, open-book, open-whatever, but they are timed quizzes. The students get twelve minutes to answer ten multiple-choice quiz questions.

The *time* was the problem for the student. He reached out to me via email and asked, "Does the school have a disability department? I'm having a hard time comprehending the quizzes in a timely manner. I need more time and would like to speak to someone in the disability office."

No biggie, I know the person who oversees the disability office quite well. In addition to contact information for the person he needed, I also asked him, "Would twenty minutes be enough time for you? I'd be happy to simply make the quizzes open for everyone for twenty minutes if that would be beneficial for you." Later that afternoon, I got an email with a certified exemption asking me to extend quiz time for this student.

Problem solved, right? Sure, but I made immediate meaning of the encounter! And not the most accurate meaning. I began to think, "My colleague is going to think I didn't do a good enough job working with this student." I wondered, "Why would my student think I was too unapproachable to work with me?" I asked, "What do I need to do to make sure my student and the school itself believe I care deeply for them and their learning experience?" One seemingly mundane encounter with so many inaccurate meanings made of it.

This kind of thing happens multiple times every day. Our shared human problem is that we usually don't make or take the time to reflect on those encounters for a plethora of reasons.

We believe this—right here, reflecting on our encounters—is the birthplace of transformation. When a person has an encounter and subsequently takes the time to reflect on that encounter, conditions are ripe for transformation to begin.

Remember Elizabeth? She is the collegiate athlete who made the protective promise that she would not be outworked. Elizabeth recently used the Brimstone Transformational Equation, and in a recent group session, she talked about an encounter she had one afternoon.

> *One day during practice, Elizabeth had an unexpected run-in with a teammate. The teammate wasn't working as hard as she was, or at least as hard as Elizabeth believed she should be. During that encounter, Elizabeth was triggered, and her emotions got the best of her. She lashed out at the teammate, yelled at her in front of the rest of the team, and left practice full of shame. The encounter negatively impacted the teammate, the team, and Elizabeth as well.*

As it turns out, this kind of thing has happened before and is a pattern of behavior for Elizabeth. Processing together with her teammates, they shared their experiences in what we call a brave space (because how safe can a space truly be when other humans are around?). We prefer to invite our clients into brave spaces because, in brave spaces, people are encouraged to take one step beyond their normal level of comfort in pursuit of the transformation they desire.

In this session, Elizabeth was able to reflect on her behavior in real time. She courageously listened, and over time, she found the equation useful. Elizabeth later reported that she could catch herself when she was triggered and then make choices. We call this transformation. We did not say that Elizabeth would respond perfectly every time in the future, but we are confident saying this is progress.

$$E + R = T$$
*Encounter + Reflection = Transformation*

Practice does not make perfect—practice makes progress! Making use of the Brimstone Transformational Equation leads to progress, which is transformation.

> Making use of the Brimstone Transformational Equation leads to progress, which is transformation.

## RESISTANCE TO REFLECTION

There are a variety of reasons people are resistant to slowing down and engaging with reflective practices. Here are a few:

### BUSYNESS IS A BADGE OF HONOR.

Kyle Kowalski of *Sloww* says, "It wasn't too long ago that 'keeping up with the Joneses' was about things—the big house, the sports car, designer clothing. But now *things* are being challenged by something 'new'—*time*." I (Kurt) have seen that shift in my own life. What used to be about what was in my possession or in my home/garage is now about how many hours I'm working compared to my peers. How many sports and activities are my kids a part of? How many boards and committees can I serve on? The "successful" American in 2025 best not appear idle! And practices like reflection often get a little too close to that feeling of being idle.

### YOU HAVE A LACK OF AWARENESS.

Contemplative Martin Laird has said, "Often, we are not even aware of how utterly dominating this inner noise is until we try to enter through the doorway of silence."[8] The inner noise of which Laird speaks can be so loud that it is both deafening and debilitating.

---

[8] Martin Laird, *Into the Silent Land: A Guide to the Christian Practice of Contemplation* (London: Oxford University Press, 2006), 4.

There's a saying, "You don't know what you don't know." And it's true, isn't it? As we've said a number of times already, many of us don't have any idea there are things to reflect on. Most of us have no idea there's another way to live our lives. So naturally, if I just plain don't know these encounters are having an impact on my life and that I actually have some say in how they affect me, it makes sense that I wouldn't engage in any sort of reflection.

We want to be clear, though—none of this makes us, or you, bad people. It frankly makes us human. Becoming aware of the benefit of reflection is really the first step to take.

## YOU DON'T KNOW HOW.

Nobel laureate and neuroscientist Santiago Ramón y Cajal (1852–1934) once said, "Every man can, if he so desires, become the sculptor of his own brain."[9] While you may not presently know how to engage in the practice of reflection, it is possible to learn techniques and practices that will have a positive impact on your life. Cajal's contention eliminates—at least for me (Chris)—the "I don't know how" argument. While it might be absolutely true that I don't know how to practice reflection today, that doesn't have to STAY true tomorrow!

Can you think of something you don't know how to do? I'm sure there are lots of things you don't know how to do. There's a lot I (Kurt) don't know how to do! One of the things I REALLY want to know how to do is to cook like a skilled chef. Sure, I can cook—kind of—but not to the skill level or, frankly, the enjoyment level I'd like to. So naturally, what do you think I do when it comes time to cook a meal? I kind of run from it. I deflect and ask my wife to cook. I default to the same old, non-risky things I DO know how to cook. I stay stuck. Sound familiar?

We all have places in our lives where we want to change, or we want

---

[9] Santiago Ramón y Cajal, *Scientific Research Rules and Advice: The Tonics of the Will* (Madrid, Spain: CSIC, 1998).

something to be different but stay stuck in what's always been. But it doesn't have to be that way. When we realize we are avoiding growth or defaulting to known and non-risky things. We can choose to do what we've always done, getting the results we've always gotten, *or* we can choose to reflect on what past encounters might be telling us about a current encounter.

## POSITIVE STEPS TOWARD CONSISTENT REFLECTION

I (Kurt) once worked in a manufacturing plant alongside a process guru. And that's not an exaggeration at all! He was literally a black belt in process improvement (look it up, I'm serious). His name was Ozzy, and Ozzy would always say that systems are perfectly designed to get the results they get—meaning if he wanted different process results, he'd have to change the process.

We think the same is true for our lives: Our lives are perfectly designed to get the results they are getting. Allow me to translate: If I want my life to be different, I have to take some tangible steps to change what I'm doing in life.

Changes like what we're proposing or adopting new habits and practices can be quite difficult and challenging to implement. But what Chris and I can say without hesitation is that when we got serious about putting things in place that helped us make reflection a part of our normal rhythm, we began to see real growth and real transformation.

We posit these tips for reflection that encourage engagement with the encounters you have:

### MAKE INTENTIONAL SPACE IN YOUR CALENDAR.

I (Chris) was in the early months of a new job when my first coach, Rodger Price, asked if I was making time for solitude and reflection—one of my stated objectives in our coaching work together. When I told him it was a struggle, his suggestion was this: "Schedule it in your calendar; everything else is scheduled, so why shouldn't that be?"

Block out a fifteen-minute window midmorning and midafternoon. Get up from your desk, move around, and check in on how you're doing:

- How have you shown up so far today?
- When did you show up in ways you don't prefer?

If fifteen minutes is too long initially, begin with five minutes. Just don't worry about the time you're taking away from work—you will make it up.

We know that scheduling time for reflection feels selfish at first, doesn't it? With so many people, projects, and other things depending on you, how can you possibly put time for reflection on the calendar?

Even fifteen minutes of reflection on a regular basis will impact all of those things depending upon you in positive ways.[10] Instead of doing those things from a "white-knuckling" posture, that time of reflection will help you do them from a place of greater clarity and intentionality.

## INVEST IN REFLECTION.

There's nothing quite like having some skin in the game. When we say, "Invest in reflection," we aren't just talking about investing your time. Buying a nice journal or paying a small fee for a good journaling app on your phone, tablet, or computer will help hold space for your planned times of reflection. One of our clients even owns a nice quill pen collection. He relishes his journaling time in this way.

Another way to think about investing in reflection is renting a space to be. Perhaps it's a cabin in a wooded area, a workspace in some niche

---

[10] James R. Bailey and Scheherazade Rehman, "Don't Underestimate the Power of Self-Reflection," *Harvard Business Review*, March 4, 2022, https://hbr.org/2022/03/dont-underestimate-the-power-of-self-reflection.

coffee shop, or a room at a monastery. When people pay for things, they are more likely to make use of them.

## KEEP A LOG OF ENCOUNTERS DAILY.

When working the "R" portion (reflection) of the Transformational Equation, it can be challenging to remember all the specifics of the "E" portion (encounter). This is especially true if the reflection is happening at the end of the day, but the encounter was on the way to work, or if you're reflecting right now on an encounter that happened last week at the family holiday gathering.

We encourage you to find a way to record or log the encounters you have as close to the encounter itself as possible. Maybe it's on your phone, either as a note or a voice memo. Maybe it's in a little notebook or journal. We know some people who actually carry a small journal with them wherever they go. Whatever your preferred method, record things like this:

- On the way to work this morning, I got cut off by a car, nearly causing an accident.
- I felt angry, out of control, and maybe even a little fearful for my safety.
- I was feeling stressed about a presentation I had to give first thing in the workday.
- I honked and wanted to display the finger (you know the one) but didn't.
- I stayed angry and stirred up the rest of the way to work but calmed down as I sat at my desk, prepping for the day.

As you record these encounters—for your own reflection, not others'—give yourself as much detail as you can. What happened? What did you feel? How did you respond? How would you rather respond? What other factors played a part? All of these are important details that will help you work E+R=T most beneficially!

## SHARE YOUR PLAN FOR REFLECTION WITH A FRIEND.

Have you ever set out to do something only to fail? We have too! Have you ever set out to do something, shared your plan with a trusted friend, and not followed through? Well, yes, we have too. However, we know that the likelihood of following through when we invite another human into our practice of intentional reflection increases greatly![11]

And maybe just to be clear, we encourage you to invite a truly trusted and safe friend into this with you. You know the friends. If they aren't going to be an encourager, maybe don't share it with them.

This sharing is less about accountability (though some really do function well with "stronger" accountability) and more about encouragement. In my experience (Kurt), I've found it extremely helpful and encouraging to have a trusted friend say, "Hey, you said you were going to devote some intentional time to reflect on the encounters you have and your response to them. How's that going?"

Let someone into the work with you.

## BE OK BEING QUIET.

Being quiet is pretty hard. At least for me (Kurt), it is! I love music of all kinds, I love a good podcast, and at certain times of the year, I LOVE listening to a live baseball game on the radio like the good Lord intended baseball to be consumed! And I'm usually always an arm's length away from my AirPods or an auxiliary cable. I can fill every moment of my day with sound that sometimes equates to nothing more than noise. One day,

---

[11] Jeff Grabmeier, "Share Your Goals—But Be Careful Whom You Tell," Ohio State News, September 3, 2019, https://news.osu.edu/share-your-goals--but-be-careful-whom-you-tell/.

however, a wise friend asked me, "How often are you just quiet?" "Never—obviously!" was my answer.

Now, don't get us wrong, there is nothing wrong with music or podcasts or baseball games, but I wonder what you might experience if you made some intentional space in your day to simply be in the quiet.

In an article on the hidden benefits of silence, Janelle Cox writes that finding moments of silence can offer us a number of physical and mental benefits. Some of those benefits include being in a space that encourages mindfulness, increasing our ability to be creative in a given moment, growing self-awareness, and even a state that encourages stimulation of our brain cells.[12] That's science!

Here's what I did: When I'd get in my car to go somewhere, I'd commit to making one of the trips (either FROM the starting point or BACK TO the starting point) with the car radio off. Did I miss out on some baseball news? Yes. Did I get behind in my podcasts? Maybe a little. Did I miss a good jam sesh in the car? Also yes. But I also gained a space in which I could think freely, not guided by the sound of what I was listening to. I could use my imagination and think about the future! I could think about how I wanted to show up to the place I was going! OR, if I wanted to, I didn't have to think at all. That's OK too! My brain needs a break as well, sometimes.

Find a time to be in the quiet and see how your brain responds.

## LISTEN TO WHAT YOUR BODY/INNER SELF IS SAYING TO YOU; DON'T RUSH TO ANSWERS.

Do you know what happens when we take time to be quiet and make time to reflect? Sometimes, nothing happens. Sometimes, the breakthrough we hope for just doesn't happen as quickly as we'd like. That's OK. Just maybe what we need in those moments is nothing more than a little slowdown.

---

[12] Janelle Cox, "The Hidden Benefits of Silence," Psych Central, April 29, 2022, https://psychcentral.com/blog/the-hidden-benefits-of-silence.

We also really do believe that if we keep putting ourselves in quiet and reflective postures, breakthrough will come! Our inner parts (more to come in Chapter Five) will help us know what they need!

You've probably heard of the book *The Body Keeps the Score* by Bessel van der Kolk, MD.[13] It's true—our bodies do keep the score of what we're carrying from encounters we've yet to resolve. But before there's a score to keep, our bodies indicate that something is going on inside us.

Tight trapezius muscles, clenched jaws, red hot ears, and many other physical indicators are like alarm bells indicating that something is stirring in us. Pay attention to those. As you reflect on encounters, begin to notice commonalities around what your physical bodies do in those situations.

Scholars and scientists all seem to agree—reflection is a skill we can learn, and its benefits are far-reaching. It seems the only thing we really have to fear—when it comes to engaging the Brimstone Transformational Equation—is fear itself. But here's the thing, friends: Making the time to reflect on your encounters will be time well spent, especially as you begin to understand some of the promises you made to yourself earlier in life, which is the focus of Chapter Four.

---

[13] Bessel van der Kolk, MD, *The Body Keeps the Score: Brain, Mind, and Body in the Healing of Trauma* (New York: Penguin, 2015).

CHAPTER

# 4

# PROMISES, PROMISES, PROMISES

*"Change is inevitable; growth is optional"*
—JOHN MAXWELL

It doesn't matter how old you are, I imagine most human beings are familiar with the phrase, "Sticks and stones may break my bones, but words will never hurt me"—you know, the 1970s phrase for telling kids to just power through painful playground experiences.

As I typed that phrase, Dwight Schrute was ringing in my ears: "FALSE!"

We know so much more today than we did fifty years ago.

Do you truly know how much power your words have? We believe your words have A LOT of power—especially the words you use when you think of yourself and who you are or the words you use when life starts to go sideways. We would even say that your words have enough power to create a picture of how you see yourself and how you see the world.

As you can imagine, sometimes, the way we see ourselves and the world can be beneficial, empowering, and productive. Other times, the way we see ourselves and the world can be harmful, disempowering, and counterproductive.

We refer to this as "meaning making." For every encounter we have, we make meaning. The meaning we make may be right, and it may be wrong—we likely have no idea regarding accuracy at the time. We make meaning, and we call these words that have the power to create a picture of ourselves and the world "promises." And when we say "create," we mean that they shape in us a reality (though it may be a perceived reality) that impacts how we show up and behave in all parts of our lives.

## HOW WE MAKE MEANING OF WORDS

One of our new learnings in recent months focuses around the idea of meaning making. Researchers continue to discover new information concerning meaning making. For instance, in a 2019 piece posted by the Business Relationship Management Institute entitled "The Neuroscience Behind Our Words," it was explained that Maria Richter and her research team found that negative words—spoken, heard, or thought—cause stress and create long-term anxiety.[14]

Let that sink in for just a moment. When we have an encounter or experience, we make meaning out of that experience. Then, we unconsciously internalize a promise to ourselves that is intended to make us feel safe in the world.

Here's the easiest example of making meaning of words we can think of. Imagine with me, if you can, that you're getting ready to move from one house to another. But man, do you need some real help! Moving is hard, and you could sure use the help of your friends on moving day. So you do what we all would do—you text them this simple message: "Hey,

---

[14] Lindsey Horton, "The Neuroscience Behind Our Words," Business Relationship Management Institute, August 8, 2019, https://brm.institute/neuroscience-behind-words/.

can you help me move next weekend?" They all say yes except for that one friend. That friend simply replies, "No, I can't."

Do you see all the meanings you could make out of that encounter? You could assume that friend doesn't like you anymore. You could assume that they're busy that day. You could assume that you did something that pushed them away. Whatever meaning you make out of it, true or not, you've just assigned a meaning to that moment that will likely lead to the internalization of a promise.

The Oxford Dictionary defines *promise* this way: "a declaration or assurance that one will do a particular thing or that a particular thing will happen." I imagine that a definition like that, or maybe even just the word "promise," stirs something up in you. You may have really strong and positive reactions to the idea of keeping your promises to people and to yourself. But others may have an equally strong negative reaction because promises made to you have been broken over and over again, causing a deep wounding.

Those are all important pieces of the puzzle that is our lives. All of those things shape who we are and how we see the world, and you'll have a chance to think a little more about them. For right now, the invitation is for you to begin to consider the promises you've made to yourself and the promises you would prefer to make to yourself for the sake of transformation.

You're probably doing the thing where you furrow your brow and curl a lip up in skepticism right now (there are many GIFs that come to mind that might illustrate the face). The concept of making promises to ourselves IS a little foreign to most of us and can be a little hard to understand—especially when we're talking about promises that were likely made years ago without our knowing it. Richter's research is useful in helping us understand that negative words release stress and anxiety-inducing hormones in human beings.[15]

A little earlier, we shared with you this idea that we all have encounters

---

[15] Maria Richter, Judith Eck, Thomas Straube, Wolfgang H.R. Miltner, and Thomas Weiss, "Do Words Hurt? Brain Activation During the Processing of Pain-Related Words," *Pain* 148 (2): 198–205, https://doi.org/10.1016/j.pain.2009.08.009.

every single day. We'd also say that we've all had significant encounters like that in our first formation—that is, the time in our lives from roughly grade school through high school.

What we know about that time in our lives is that those are the years in which we are first being formed (hence "first formation") in deep and meaningful ways, for better or for worse. Our minds start to cement and lock in the ways we see authority, relationships with others, and the world more broadly. We make meaning of every encounter, especially the confusing, negative, and painful ones.

Why do we do this? It's simple. Our younger, first-formation brains often don't have the capability to think abstractly, so we often assign the simplest meaning possible.

Let's take our friend, Jack, for instance. Having settled into married life and beginning to climb the corporate ladder, Jack found himself in an important meeting with some company executives. He had climbed through the ranks fairly quickly and was a bright, shining star in the company. He was in line for a promotion, but in this meeting, he noticed what he thought was a frown on one of the executive's faces during the meeting, and he spiraled.

Jack lost all sense of confidence, no longer came across as capable and confident, and missed out on the promotion. He was moving along just fine, felt safe at the top of the hamster wheel—until he didn't—and wound up stuck in the same role for the next five years.

This is where our conversation about promises begins!

## PROTECTIVE PROMISES

It's likely that the first promise we made to ourselves is a *protective promise*. And you guessed it—this was a promise that began as a way to keep ourselves safe. That's really what this is about, isn't it? Remember the hamster wheel? The origin of our protective promise is truly rooted in our deep desire and deep instinct to be safe and to make sure our needs get met.

Practically speaking, it might go like this: The younger first-formation version of ourselves had a painful encounter with our world. And in order to keep that pain from being repeated, you guessed it, we promised ourselves that we would never allow ourselves to feel that way again.

One client of ours, whom we'll call Jen, had a profoundly painful experience when she was in grade school. And for Jen, the pain of this experience was wrapped up with the feeling of being embarrassed. At a crucial time in her life, Jen had something happen to her that caused her classmates (for her, it felt like EVERY classmate) to laugh at her in ways that were unwelcome.

Jen's protective promise was, "I will never allow myself to be embarrassed again."

Certainly, Jen didn't know she was making that promise at that moment. It was only many years later, as she engaged in her own self-discovery, that she realized that was a promise she'd made to the younger version of herself. But it was in that moment of embarrassment, and dealing with the fallout of it, that her autonomic nervous system went into hyperdrive to make sure that promise was kept, no matter what!

For me (Kurt), in addition to the protective promise I shared earlier, I made this promise: "Don't ever stand out for any reason." I can trace that a long way back to my first formation and see that it has its roots in the way my family would talk about people we'd see who had lots of tattoos or piercings. Or maybe they had brightly dyed hair or wore bright clothing that was deemed weird. I heard those statements come out of my family, none of which were kind or gracious, and I learned that I didn't want people to say those things about me. So the easiest way to do that was to "never stand out."

For me (Chris), walking into a room full of strangers makes me want to run for cover. I am tempted to list off a bunch of things I would rather do instead of walking into a room full of strangers, but the word count is growing too long. That's how much I dislike "mixer" activities. For the longest time, I had no idea why, but discovering protective promises has changed my life.

When I was in middle school, Friday nights in the fall meant going to the high school football game. Being at the high school football game but not on the field meant there was a good game going on behind the bleachers, and I have to tell you, that was usually the better of the two games going on.

Inevitably, however, a fight would break out in the game behind the bleachers, and one night, that fight included me. Everyone behind the bleachers circled around us—me and the girl who was bigger and stronger than my scrawny self. Now, I grew up in a day and age when boys did not hit girls, so I took my lumps, and the reality is, I would have taken my lumps anyway because she was bigger and stronger than me.

The protective promise, "I will not be controlled," may have been born that night. I was humiliated and had nowhere to go with the embarrassment, the hurt, and the pain. And here's the thing. While I have never shared this story before, I am present to the fact that every time I find myself surrounded, those feelings come rushing back.

I did my level best from that night forward to not allow myself to be surrounded or to be controlled again. Unfortunately, there was another time or two when I found myself surrounded and out of my element.

Neither Kurt nor I share these stories to elicit sympathy but rather to share the impact that first-formation experiences and the resulting protective promises can have in our lives.

## PROTECTIVE PROMISES START WITH A REAL NEED

There's one important thing we should say about protective promises. At the time, in our first formation, we NEEDED the protection those promises offered. And frankly, at the time we made them, they were often quite effective in keeping us safe.

Jen NEEDED to be safe around her classmates. I NEEDED to feel safe in my family of origin. Chris NEEDED to not find himself surrounded or controlled again.

In this way, protective promises are not bad or harmful—at least, they didn't start out that way. The trouble is that they hang on for years, and they start to form an autopilot way of being in us that isn't really the truest version of us. Or maybe said differently, the autopilot causes us to behave, react, and respond in ways we may not love. Our autonomic nervous system gets so good at protecting us that it just keeps protecting us, even if we don't actually need the protection anymore.

Sir Isaac Newton (this is hopefully the last physics lesson in these pages) said that an object in motion will stay in motion until it is acted upon by an outside force. We think protective promises work in the same way. Once we form them, get good at living them out, and see their benefits (or perceived benefits), we just keep on allowing them to drive the bus of our lives unchecked and unchallenged.

> Our autonomic nervous system gets so good at protecting us that it just keeps protecting us, even if we don't actually need the protection anymore.

This is true of us, of you, of your neighbor Cynthia next door, and of all humans. Please hear us say that the truth of this in your life does not make you a bad person. It makes you human.

Let's play our previous examples out a little bit. Jen had protected herself from embarrassment for so long she didn't even know she was doing it. She did, however, know she was holding back during meetings. She calculated every public move and word she delivered. She realized there certainly may have been times she misstepped and said something out loud that wasn't 100 percent accurate. Jen might swing a golf club and send a golf ball at a 180-degree angle into the woods from a tee box in front of her friends. But what was also true was that adult Jen, in adult situations, was very unlikely to be laughed at like grade school Jen experienced. The danger simply wasn't what it once was, so the protection didn't need to be either.

Think about my (Kurt's) protective promise that I'd never ever stand out. Truthfully, I hadn't uncovered that promise until fairly recently as I wrestled with why I didn't want to wear my red sneakers (yes, I'm a sneakerhead) in public.

Or maybe I began to realize something wasn't right when I felt some strong internal resistance to walking into an overnight staff retreat in a fully furnished and stocked Airbnb carrying my own pillow from home. What might the other staff think?!

The reality is that I, as adult Kurt, realized the danger of being seen in red sneakers or carrying my own pillow to a place full of pillows was simply not what it once was, so neither did my protections need to be.

Interestingly enough, Chris now finds himself in a weekly meeting where people gather in a circle to talk about the details that lie ahead as he and a group of people prepare to serve others. The danger that existed under those Friday night lights or in the city park on his walk home from school is not present in his current situations.

Even the banquet he went to recently didn't present the same kind of danger for Chris. In real time, he could feel all the feels his eleven-year-old self felt behind the bleachers, looked over his shoulder a time or two, trying to remain on the outside of the circle, but "I will not be controlled," and everything that accompanies that, did not need to surface.

So here's the punch line after all that.

The protective promise creates an autopilot that ultimately drives the bus of our lives when it comes to how we show up in the world, and it is likely driving the bus in directions that are not in line with who we really are today. Instead of helping us become our truest and most authentic selves today, protective promises keep us stuck all the way back in our first formation. And, friends, the world doesn't need six-year-old Chris, seventh-grade Kurt, or whatever earlier version of you that your promises have you stuck in. The world needs all of our truest and most authentic selves today!

The world NEEDS Jen's voice in those meetings! The world NEEDS

Kurt to express himself fully and honestly. And the world NEEDS Chris to relinquish control, to not be on the defensive, and to be fully present to the people he is with.

## THE EFFECT OF MEMORIES ON PROTECTIVE PROMISES

One of the major challenges to moving beyond our protective promises is the human memory. Ribot's Law explains that older memories are more stable than newer ones.[16] It's why the protective promise from our first formation is so powerful and difficult to conquer.

French psychologist Theodore Ribot noted this all the way back in 1882. Ribot's Law explains why Alzheimer's patients can vividly remember the events of the summer of 1962 but can't remember what they were told an hour ago.

> Past behaviors that seemed helpful at the time were indeed helpful at the time, and they are difficult to replace.

The point we want to make is that past behaviors that seemed helpful at the time were indeed helpful at the time, and they are difficult to replace. This is why the transformational journey really matters. Retracing our steps and evaluating the meaning we made in our first formation may set the table for us to train ourselves to behave in ways that are more purposeful and preferred.

We suggest engaging in the practice of guided solitude as a way to engage your own first-formation encounters. Please feel free to use the prompts on the following pages as you engage the "R" (reflection) in the Transformational Equation.

---

[16] "Ribot's Law," APA Dictionary, https://dictionary.apa.org/ribots-law.

## REFLECTION: UNCOVERING PROTECTIVE PROMISES

1. Spend some time in silence and reflection. Find a peaceful place, put your phone or devices away, and pay attention to your posture. As you do so, what do you feel in your body? In your heart? In your mind?

2. Think back to your childhood. Consider as many positive experiences from your first formation (up to ten) as you can remember.

3. Still thinking about your childhood, record as many negative experiences as come to mind from your childhood.

4. Finally, what do you wish you had experienced or learned that you didn't experience or learn in your first formation?

5. As you think about transitioning from protective promises to more purposeful and preferred ones, what do you want to say to the younger you?

6. Taking your time and remembering to be both curious and compassionate with yourself, recall a time when you made meaning—meaning that has led to negative behavior and a protective promise.

7. Spend some time with this meaning, journaling thoughts and feelings that stir in you. What protective promise did you make?

8. Sitting with that protective promise, list any and every emotion or feeling that stirs in you. Feel free to return to the homework often.

## PURPOSEFUL PROMISES

We have shown the power of the human brain, the power of memory, and the power of words throughout this book. We've even helped you understand the power of the protective promises made to ourselves in our first formation.

The meaning we made out of experiences we had during those first-formation encounters caused a need for us to experience the feeling of safety, resulting in a protective promise. That protective promise was useful at the time, but as months, years, and decades have passed, the protective promise is now, at best, no longer useful and, at worst, inappropriate.

The autonomic nervous system stores the feelings of those experiences, and we often react without even thinking—what we and others refer to as an "autopilot" way of being. When something happens that triggers those emotions, feelings, and thoughts, we simply get into action.

Every human being does this. One of the reasons we do this is noted in Ribot's Law. Older memories are more stable than new ones. Because this is true and because humans also have a hard time converting short-term memory into long-term memory, we encourage the intentional process of replacing those protective promises with *purposeful promises.*

Allow us to explain this in just a bit more detail by way of example. A movie released in 2000 called *Memento* told the story of Leonard Shelby, who suffered from anterograde amnesia, a condition that made it impossible for him to convert short-term memory into long-term memory.[17]

In order to remember the things necessary for him to carry on his mission, Shelby had words and phrases tattooed on his body as reminders. David Eagleman explains that all human beings do this. "We etch the critical *where-have-I-been* information into our neural circuitry rather than our skin," he says. "This is how our future selves know what we've been

---

[17] *Memento*, directed by Christopher Nolan (Summit Entertainment, 2000), 1:53, https://www.imdb.com/title/tt0209144/.

through and thereby what to do next."[18] We are not insinuating that you have to tattoo a purposeful promise on your body, though it has been done (right, Kurt?).

> When people learn new pieces of information, the structure of the brain actually changes.

We share this information as an indicator that change is possible. Many people we work with are cynical and resigned to the fact that they will never be able to behave in a different manner, but neuroscience seems to be catching up with the Apostle Paul, who said, "Do not conform to the pattern of this world, but be transformed by the renewing of your mind" (Romans 12:2). Recent research actually backs up this biblical principle, showing that when people learn new pieces of information, the structure of the brain actually changes.

"The elaborate pattern of connections in the brain—the circuitry—is full of life: connections between neurons ceaselessly blossom, die, and reconfigure. You are a different person than you were at this time last year because the gargantuan tapestry of your brain has woven itself into something new."[19] All this to say that transformation is possible.

Let's walk this out just a little bit. When I (Chris) found myself behind the bleachers on that particular Friday night, surrounded and pummeled as an eleven-year-old boy by that girl who is still likely bigger and stronger than I am, I made lots of meaning. As a result, I made the protective promise (unconsciously) that "I will not be controlled." The way that protective promise manifested itself was in lots of unhealthy ways. In order to try to experience the feeling of safety, I did everything I could to not be surrounded anymore, but I also lashed out at people, ran my mouth a lot, and sought safety in other experiences.

In adulthood, when I felt ganged up on and that protective promise

---

[18] Eagleman, *Livewired*, 208–209.

[19] Eagleman, *Livewired*, 8.

resulted in me being combative or reactive in a meeting, I could not access my best thinking and be curious with myself. After more than a decade of understanding my protective promise and numerous attempts at creating a purposeful promise that is more useful in my mid-fifties, I finally have a purposeful promise that serves me far better:

"It's okay, and I'm okay."

I have written numerous iterations of this purposeful promise. It began with a lot of church-ese because that was what I thought was expected of me. "By the grace of God, I am who I am" was my initial purposeful promise. While true, it did not stop me from doing the things I do when I am triggered, so edit upon edit was made.

The power of writing out a new purposeful promise is akin to Leonard Shelby tattooing critical information onto his body so he wouldn't forget his mission. My new purposeful promise rewires the neural circuitry of my brain in ways that remind me of the past while giving me the agency to behave more purposefully today.

Lucy can say the same thing. Lucy grew up in a day and age when women did not challenge men. Her father was domineering and, as we previously explained, Lucy was expected to be perfect. She was not allowed to talk back, challenge, or question male authority. Lucy made the meaning that she had no value and made the protective promise, "I stay quiet because my thoughts don't matter."

After getting clear on her protective promise and growing in her understanding of who she is as a human being, Lucy is more emotionally mature now, and she has a purposeful promise that helps her engage with male authority. Her new purposeful promise, "My voice matters," now enables her to ask her husband to give her a chance to speak. This more purposeful promise enables Lucy to manage herself in board meetings with male authority figures and in her family of origin as well.

I (Kurt) appreciate Chris's willingness to write a paragraph in these pages that includes "I have never shared this before." What a helpful modeling of vulnerability! As I mentioned above, the protective promise,

"Don't stand out," has been a recent finding. But it's also been an incredibly hard promise to move beyond. Why? I think it's because I'm a highly relational human.

Underneath all my protective promises is really the fear that you, or someone else, might withdraw from me relationally. That is the worst possible outcome in my mind when these promises start up. And it doesn't just feel like a "possible outcome"—it feels like a guaranteed outcome! So that protective promise led to all sorts of behaviors that really sought to keep relationships in place and healthy (ironic, I know). Most of those behaviors were not sustainable.

That protective promise needed to go, and I needed to do the work to establish a more true and purposeful promise to replace it. Remember, protective promises don't simply go away; they need to be replaced in our brains.

So I went to work and slowly began to uncover what I had just shared about the fear of relational withdrawal. All that hard work led me to this purposeful promise: "I am worthy of being in relationships with others just as I am."

Does that mean nobody will ever look at my red sneakers and say, "Look at that weirdo!" No, of course not. In fact, it probably happens quite often . . . they're VERY red! But "I am worthy of being in relationships with others just as I am" is still true.

As I've lived that purposeful promise out slowly, progressively, day by day, I see that it's true of me as a human being, and it's also been affirmed by those in my life with whom I value the deepest relationship.

The best purposeful promises are clear, passionate, and powerful. Purposeful promises avoid using words and phrases like "I will" or "I might." We believe this to be so because the most powerful, purposeful promises are ultimately grounded in truth.

In making the purposeful promise, we are committing ourselves to new ways of being. Because we are often behaving our way into new ways of thinking, we cannot allow circumstances to drive the bus. We need our best thinking to drive the bus, so we PROMISE to do something. We don't question it—we declare it!

As Abraham Joshua Heschel once wrote, "Speech has power. Words do not fade. What starts out as a sound ends in a deed." The point is when we say something or declare we are going to do something, that word becomes a deed. This new, purposeful promise is a conscious, intentional announcement of a new way of addressing issues that arrive in our lives.

> This new, purposeful promise is a conscious, intentional announcement of a new way of addressing issues that arrive in our lives.

## REFLECTION: WRITING A PURPOSEFUL PROMISE

Writing a Purposeful Promise will be similar to the process of uncovering your protective promise. We invite you to find a quiet place, connect yourself to your breathing and the ground beneath your feet, and ask yourself some questions:

1. Spend some time in silence and reflection. Find a peaceful place, put your phone or devices away, and pay attention to your posture. As you do so, what do you feel in your body? In your heart? In your mind?

2. Do you feel resigned or cynical that change is possible? If so, what do you believe the resistance is about?

3. Spending time in silence and reflection, think back on any experience from your first formation where you created a protective promise. Are there meanings you made in those encounters that you might see differently today?

4. What possible positive meanings can you make? List at least two other possibilities.

5. Having considered these meanings, make and take the time to create a purposeful promise. Write it out and take it with you wherever you go.

5. Is there someone you can share this purposeful promise with? Who is it? Text or call them to set up a time to share it with them in person or on a Zoom or Facetime call.

6. Finally, spend a little more time in reflection and allow yourself to be present to what you are learning. Journal whatever comes to the surface for you here as you think about leaving the protective promise behind and lean into your new, purposeful promise.

7. Return to the homework throughout the week.

## PREFERRED PROMISES

You're two-thirds of the way through the journey of replacing the protective promises you made to yourself all those years ago. Way to go! You've journeyed much further than many adults ever do! The *Harvard Business Review* has stated that only 15 percent of Americans consider themselves to be "self-aware."[20] You're doing it! Keep going!

> Your words have power, especially in creating a path forward on this journey of transformation into a new way of being.

That brings us to the way forward. You have read "your words have power" multiple times, but let us say it one more time. *Your words have power*, especially in creating a path forward on this journey of transformation into a new way of being.

Have you ever heard the phrase, "A person without direction is like a ship without a rudder"? You've probably heard some version of that phrase that was first said by Scottish philosopher Thomas Carlyle.[21]

Now, I (Kurt) will admit that I am NO sailor, nor am I a boat expert, but I understand what he's saying. A ship without a rudder is unable to be steered. It simply moves on the water in whatever direction and bearing that the wind and the current dictate at any given moment. It doesn't take a maritime expert to see the problem of a ship without a rudder.

While there are lots of ways to define "direction" in Carlyle's quote (so many we could probably write a book on just answering THAT question),

---

[20] Craig Dickerson, "The Ladder of Inference: Building Self-Awareness to Be a Better Human-Centered Leader," Harvard Business Publishing Corporate Learning, May 9, 2024, https://www.harvardbusiness.org/the-ladder-of-inference-building-self-awareness-to-be-a-better-human-centered-leader/#_edn1.

[21] Thomas Carlyle, Henry Duff Traill, and Oliver Cromwell, *Sartor Resartus* (London: Chapman, 1897).

we believe that preferred promises are the promises that move us or steer us, if you will, toward our preferred way of being.

Instead of living into an old and outdated protective promise, now our purposeful promise helps us intentionally replace that protective promise and use more intentional and purposeful words to live into the way we prefer to BE when we find ourselves triggered.

Notably, these new preferred promises remind us of how we've chosen to be, not only when it's easy to do so but maybe more impactfully when it's hard to do so.

Another way to think about preferred promises is to imagine them as being similar to guiding principles. These promises are based on the beliefs and values we've identified as important to us. There is a difference, however, between a guiding principle and a preferred promise. A preferred promise is strong and, dare I say, binding. It's clear and compelling. It's something that is free from condition and is, on some level, aspirational in the sense that it may challenge us.

I (Kurt) have talked about the protective promise that for a long time said, "Don't stand out." My preferred promise that addresses that is short and concise: "I express myself honestly and authentically." Easy peasy, right?

Well, allow us to invoke the words of the wise twentieth-century philosopher (I love this), Mike Tyson, and this deeply profound quote: "Everyone has a plan until they get punched in the mouth."[22] It's true, isn't it? At least our experience would say it's true. Mostly, I'd say it's true that we do, in fact, get punched in the mouth multiple times daily.

Sometimes, our lives feel like repeated punches in the mouth! You know the times. The times when your kids just seem to be sick all the time. The times when you can't seem to meet a deadline at work. The times when your car breaks down at the worst possible time. The times when it

---

[22] Mike Tyson, "Mike Tyson: Everyone Has a Plan Until They Get Punched in the Mouth," MMA Source, YouTube, 6:05, https://www.youtube.com/watch?v=qSuMgOu8QPo.

feels like the world is just out to get you at every turn. It's at THOSE times we think preferred promises are so important.

If we're all honest with ourselves, choosing a new way of being is pretty easy when it's not challenged by anyone or anything. The trouble is, that is just not real life. Living into a new way of being IS about doing so while getting punched in the mouth.

How WILL you be when your kids are sick all the time? How WILL you be when deadlines aren't met? How WILL you be when your car breaks down? These are the situations when the real fruit of transformation lies!

I (Kurt) am a people pleaser from WAY back! And one of the things that's true about me in my people-pleasing state is that I can be prone to not telling the whole truth or at least withholding the whole truth if the danger of disappointment crops up. So, over the course of the last couple of years, I've adopted this preferred promise: "I tell the truth." Notice, it's not "I tell the truth when everyone's OK with it" or "I tell the truth to the level people can handle it." No. I tell the truth.

Frankly, it's always been easy to tell the truth when the consequences of telling the truth are minimal or when the truth will bring joy to the hearer or connectedness to the relationship. It's always been much harder to tell the whole truth when the hearer might not be super in love with what I'm saying. Just recently, someone in my orbit made a decision that had a serious impact on me. I had the opportunity to say, "It's OK, don't worry about it," but that's not the truth of how I was feeling. Instead, with "I tell the truth" at the top of my mind, I shared calmly, thoughtfully, and truthfully the anger I was feeling and the impact their actions had on me.

That's what preferred promises do. They chart new actions that replace the old autopilot that drove the bus of our lives for so long.

Here's the asterisk in all this.

Does crafting and living into a really thoughtful preferred promise mean we'll never show up in the old protective ways again? No. Absolutely not. Because you are human, you will have times when you revert back to those old, protective ways of being.

Think about it: You've likely spent decades protecting yourself. It will take a lot of intentionally choosing your preferred promise to truly replace your old ways.

But here's the beauty of a preferred promise. Failing to keep that promise to yourself is not an occasion to feel shame. It's not the time to say, "See, I knew I couldn't be different." Rather, it's an occasion to say to yourself, "Self, I'm sorry that I didn't keep that promise. The impact of that is real. Now, I promise anew, armed with the learning that comes in not keeping my word."

Let's talk about Jen. Jen's preferred promise is "I let the world see me at the level I choose." Remember, for so many years (again, literal decades), everything in her protected her from being embarrassed like she was in grade school. It would be wildly unrealistic to believe that she'd simply never protect herself again after making her preferred promise.

But what's not wildly unrealistic is that NOW Jen can notice, "I didn't show up as fully 'me' in that meeting." And she does! We celebrate that with Jen. And Jen knows this isn't a time to beat herself up for not keeping her promise to herself; it's a time to exercise self-compassion and apologize to herself, followed by the renewing of her promise.

Friends, there are few things more beautiful than this sort of interaction!

But there's one more thing we want to say about preferred promises. You, like us, will need to create multiple preferred promises that can be employed in whatever given situation you find yourselves in. Different circumstances will demand different preferred promises.

We have mentioned we like to spend time on our bicycles. While that's true, we also know that time spent on our bicycles means that we spend time on the correct bicycle for the ride we're on.

If I (Kurt) want to hit some sick single-track gnar (yes, that's a real term, trust me), I would never pack a road bike to do so. It wouldn't just be nearly impossible to do so—it would also be a terrible time. The same is true when Chris wants to grind some miles on the road; he would never go to the bike shop and rent a mountain bike. For maximum effectiveness, fun, and training purposes, we need the proper bike for a given ride.

The same is true for preferred promises. We go through every day finding ourselves in a WIDE array of situations. We have interactions with spouses and children, our family of origin, our boss, our direct reports, our friends, and the list could go on and on. It's likely that each of these unique interactions and relationships stirs up unique things in us, requiring unique and intentional responses.

For example, most of us respond differently to an anxiety-stirring conversation with our supervisor than we do with one of the members of our family of origin. It's likely the difference in response is connected to a different protection happening in us, but no matter what the reason for the difference is, we'll be most likely to show up how we prefer when we're prepared to experience those differences.

One of the best ways to be prepared to respond with a preferred promise is by being curious with ourselves before the moments happen. One of our favorite questions to ask is, "What's the threat?" I (Chris) usually follow that question up with this one: "Am I going to die?" The question Kurt likes to ask that I love the most is this: "What is true (about the threat)?"

I love this question on so many levels. Our protective promise is often born out of a lie, but being able to ask, "What is true?" has helped to shape many conversations and enabled me to show up using one of my preferred promises because I've been prepared in advance.

For instance, when I walk into a meeting where I imagine my leadership is going to be challenged or questioned, I can be ready. Rather than reacting or responding from a place of defensiveness or believing the lie that I am not a good leader, I can respond from a place of security because I have a preferred promise about leadership: "I lead with authenticity, integrity, and courage; that makes me a person worth following."

When I am prepared in advance, that preferred promise stops me from responding negatively almost every time. So does my preferred promise about relationships.

Let's face it, relationships come and go. Friendships come into our lives for a season, and then someone else does. At times, relationships can be painful, and if we aren't careful, we choose comfort over relationships and choose to isolate ourselves.

Early in my (Chris) married life, we were friends with teachers. One of our friend couples moved away, and then a second did too. My spouse and I made a verbal agreement that we would not befriend teachers anymore.

After a couple of moves, we have now lived in the same community since 1999, and guess what? Our best friends are teachers! During those times when we feel like we aren't loveable or worthy of friendships, I hold onto this preferred promise: "I give deeply in relationships because it is better to love and be hurt than to never love at all."

Promises, promises, promises. We hope you have come to understand how powerful our words and memories are and have a sense of just how useful intentionally purposeful and preferred promises can be in altering the trajectory of your life.

Before we transition to another resource for thinking about our inner life, we would be remiss if we didn't provide you with a guided solitude opportunity to create your own preferred promises.

## REFLECTION: CRAFTING YOUR PREFERRED PROMISE

1. Spend some time in silence and solitude, thinking back on your life. If you could name some of the beliefs or values that have driven your life, what would they be?

2. You have been introduced to Protective Promises and Preferred Promises. You are in the process of behaving your way into new ways of being. Here, please spend some time considering a lie you once believed about yourself. How would you prefer to be? Make and take the time to write out a preferred promise.

4. This time, consider a situation where you often respond in ways you later regret. Let's say you make a mistake on the job, and your supervisor is angry with you. How do you typically behave? How do you want to behave next time? Write a preferred promise for this situation.

5. Create a preferred promise for yourself for the following situations:

As an employee:

As a teammate or coworker:

When you receive a compliment:

When you succeed:

When you fail:

CHAPTER

# 5

# WELCOMING ALL PARTS OF YOURSELF

*No amount of self-improvement can make up for a lack of self-acceptance.*
—ROBERT HOLDEN

We've covered a lot of ground to this point in pursuit of providing you with ways to understand why you do what you do when you do what you do. We've even helped you see that we all do something when we do what we do. There is strength in numbers, we suppose, or at least some sense of solidarity in not being in this alone.

The reality is we all have encounters, and we make meaning out of those experiences, as we've thoroughly explained. We've shared some of the neuroscience behind this truth, and we've also explained how both our words and memories play a part in how we show up in the world.

If you are like us, you might feel shame or disgust with parts of yourself. That's a powerful statement, and it's stated powerfully on purpose for a purpose. These parts of us do what they do, not to expose us but to help us avoid feeling the pain we previously experienced, often in our first formation.

There is a *true self* alive in each of us. When our true self is in control, our best thinking enables us to behave in thoughtful ways. We respond with our best thinking, we behave in ways we choose to behave, and we are most fully ourselves when the true self is active.

Unfortunately, there are other times when our protective promise is activated, and parts of us do what they do when they do what they do.

I (Chris) am a very competitive person. Competing and achieving success is what I did early in my first formation to keep others from thinking or finding out that I was worthless. I can even go so far as to say competing and achieving is what I did as a way of not being controlled.

This "way of being" followed me into high school, college, and all the way into adulthood. It was not always bad to be competitive and achieve success. Hear me when I say competing and working to be successful are not bad traits. The problem, for us, is found in the *motivations* for the competitive spirit.

As I made the transition from competitor to father of the competitor—or even fan of my teams—that competitive switch would still be tripped. As father of the competitor, however, I had no say in what was happening on the basketball court or the football field. I was also a business owner and, later, engaged in full-time ministry. I would leave games full of regret and remorse and say things like, "I hate that part of me. I wish that competitive thing in me would just go away."

Have you ever had a similar experience? Your experience may not have anything to do with athletics or competing, but have you ever said, "I hate that part of me"?

We get it, and we want to help you see that it is possible to welcome all parts of yourself.

> **It is possible to welcome all parts of yourself.**

In this chapter, we'd like to introduce you to the theory first introduced by Dr. Richard Schwartz—the internal family systems (IFS) theory. We have found

IFS helpful in our own transformational journeys and offer concepts for you to consider. (This chapter in no way replaces work with an IFS therapist but rather provides another lens through which we can view those pesky, first-formation encounters you had.) And fortunately, if you've ever seen Disney's *Inside Out* or *Inside Out 2*, you're already at a 101 level with the basics of IFS!

## IFS THEORY AND PROTECTIVE PROMISES

The contention of IFS is that all human beings are made up of parts. The part of us that is thoughtful and fully alive is the true self. The true self expresses itself calmly, with clarity, compassion, confidence, connection, courage, creativity, and curiosity.

There are also parts of us that get into action when our protective promise is triggered—these are known as *protector parts*. The work of the protectors is to get into action to keep us from feeling all the feels that played an important role in creating our exiled parts—the parts of us we try to avoid at all costs. It's important to understand that the intention of the protectors is good.

In IFS, there are no bad parts, just parts that are seeking to protect us or meet a fundamental need.

In my protective promise example behind the bleachers, the exiled part of me was pushed down deep inside because I felt anger, fear, shame, and despair as a result of the experience of being surrounded and pummeled.

> In IFS, there are no bad parts, just parts that are seeking to protect us or meet a fundamental need.

For me (Kurt), my creative part was exiled early on in life. That same protector that created the protective promise, "Don't ever stand out," also suppressed and exiled the part of me that would allow me to express myself creatively. Expression and creativity—at least in times where those things might create a spot where I'd stand out—felt dangerous. And protectors are really good at protecting!

Similar to the meaning we made that led to our protective promises, these exiled parts were unconsciously pushed deep inside so we wouldn't have to engage them again. Into adulthood, however, when those feelings of the exiled part were threatened, their protectors got into action. There are two types of protector parts—managers and firefighters.

Managers are the parts of us that strive to anticipate and prevent difficult situations from happening. Managers control the situation, doing what they can to control what is going on internally as well as what goes on outside of us. When my fear of failure (Chris) is activated, the manager part gets into action and pushes me to succeed.

Firefighters, on the other hand, are reactive. Anger and Rage are two of my firefighters. When I competed, and when I watched my kids compete, the injustice of terrible calls by officials often hit my exiled part. Their calls were going to negatively impact results, and people were going to equate my team losing with thinking or finding out that I (or my team) was worthless.

When that exiled part is triggered, the firefighter Rage lashed out at referees. Anger often muttered under my breath when others made mistakes, even my own children, all for the sake of trying to protect my exiled parts. Again, the intent of our protective parts is good. Their actions and results may say otherwise, but their intent is good.

The work of IFS is to be able to identify each part of us and to welcome them with love. When we can see them for what they are—not as right or wrong, nor as good or bad, but simply as parts of a life we've lived and have developed over time—a reality of opportunity exists.

As is the case in all meaning making and subsequent promise creation, there are healthy parts in IFS. These parts of ourselves are aspects of our personality that embody aspirations, qualities, and resources that are found in the truest version of ourselves. Unfortunately, these healthy parts are often overshadowed at best (eclipsed at worst) by the intense work of our protector parts and the deep pain of our exiled parts.

For me (Chris), realizing that Anger and Rage were trying to help was a good thing. It enabled me to welcome them, not hate them, and to thank them for trying to protect me.

My true self can also welcome "Competitor," the manager part of me that is always trying to help me avoid the feeling of worthlessness and invite that part to relax and let it know, "It's okay, and I'm okay." This is what enables me to be okay each week when I stand around in a circle with people I am leading, free of anxiety and fear. My true self is in control of the situation, and I do not have to be on guard.

> Realizing that Anger and Rage were trying to help was a good thing. It enabled me to welcome them, not hate them, and to thank them for trying to protect me.

I (Kurt) find the idea that my parts, even the parts I used to deem unhelpful or bad, are really, earnestly trying to help me is a deep and profound revelation in my life and transformation journey. And they are doing their best to help me.

One of my most overworked managers is what I call the "Calculator." No, not my TI-83 calculator (my fellow late eighties kids will get that one)—the kind of calculator that is always trying to look one step ahead so that it can plan actions and words in such a way that the people around me might not begin to think that I'm incompetent.

My most called upon firefighter is called "Self-deprecator." Why? I think it's because when the danger of looking incompetent gets past "Calculator," "Self-deprecator" needs to step in and put the fire out. Often, the "Self-deprecator" part will do that by prefacing sentences with, "Well, this probably isn't good or right or what you're looking for, etc." Maybe you've done that.

But welcoming them in compassionately, listening to what they have to say, and inviting them to see that the danger isn't as real as it once was allows me to show up authentically as my true self (that part of me that's been exiled), not calculating or self-deprecating.

## DISCOVERING BRUCE'S PROTECTIVE PARTS

Meeting with Bruce recently, I (Chris) was able to share the theory of IFS with him, explaining the impact of protector and exiled parts. Remember Bruce, our friend from the introduction—the successful person who also struggles to believe that he matters? With the new realization that the true self is the best self and that the protector parts are not bad—they are just trying to protect us from our pain—Bruce and I could prepare for the next time Distancer showed up.

This is where we think IFS and promises dovetail so well. Bruce is beginning to see how he can create a preferred promise that will allow him to graciously notice and welcome Distancer when he shows up at Bruce's next gathering. Bruce is also working on creating that preferred promise that will allow his truest self to share his beliefs and thoughts, even when he may be the only one in the group who holds them. As he talked about the struggle he was having to find a place where he was okay being himself in a group of people, I invited Bruce to consider what the protector part was.

Bruce sat silently before me for a while, thinking about the question. With his eyes closed, Bruce calmly welcomed his manager part into the space. Distancer is the part of Bruce that gets into action when he feels discomfort in a group setting. Remember, the manager part wants to control the situation and protect Bruce from having to feel his exiled part—the part that made the meaning that his opinions and beliefs don't matter—and, as a result, that he doesn't matter.

As he identified Distancer, I asked Bruce what was happening in his mind while he was meeting with the group. Bruce explained the conversation with the group had taken a turn that he disagreed with. He told me there were seven or eight other people in the conversation, and he was struggling to know what to do.

I then asked Bruce to ask Distancer what he was doing there. "I'm here to help you gracefully leave the meeting," Distancer told Bruce.

Sitting there quietly, still with his eyes closed, I asked Bruce if there was anything else he could see Distancer doing. "He's beginning to get up from the table," Bruce said.

"What usually happens when Distancer gets up from the table?" I asked Bruce.

"I leave the meeting and feel like a failure because I let my belief that 'I don't matter' force me to leave the meeting."

Bruce and I continued a conversation in this way, bouncing questions and answers back and forth about how he was feeling in this meeting and how he saw Distancer in the middle of it all. I finally asked this question: "What if you thank Distancer for being with you and ask him to take a break, explaining that you don't need him to work so hard for you right now?"

A tear was followed by a second and then a third as Bruce considered the question.

"What are the tears about, Bruce?" I asked.

"I didn't know I could ask him to take a break! I thought this was just how I had to be."

As we've already said, our intention with wading into these IFS waters is not to make you an IFS expert. Shoot, we're not even IFS experts per se. Rather, the intent is to help you understand that you are not your full self, and we are not our whole selves, as long as exiled parts remain unwelcomed into

> You are not your full self, and we are not our whole selves, as long as exiled parts remain unwelcomed into the full self and the protectors are compassionately invited to take a break from their striving.

the full self and the protectors are compassionately invited to take a break from their striving.

So keep digging. Keep learning. Find some IFS resources for yourself. Again, we really do believe that the promises work we're inviting you to do—while understanding the basics of IFS in your pocket—is as close to a "secret sauce" as one can get when talking about the transformational journey!

## REFLECTION: WELCOMING ALL PARTS OF YOURSELF

1. Create some space to engage in a time of silence and solitude. With pen and paper at hand, write down any parts of yourself that you aren't fond of.

   Are there traits that make you feel embarrassed?

   Are there things you do that cause you to feel shame?

   Write down all that come to mind.

2. Once you have identified those parts, see if you can assign motivation to their behavior.

   Are the firefighters trying to protect you by reacting to a threat?

   Are the managers trying to protect you by anticipating and preventing painful experiences?

3. As you categorize your protector parts, can you start to see the exiled part that they are protecting you from?

   How would you describe that exiled part?

What emotions and feelings are connected to it?

Is there a connection to a protective promise?

4. How might you begin to think about welcoming all parts of yourself?

5. Is there anything in your way from accepting all parts of yourself?

CHAPTER

# 6

# ONCE YOU SEE IT, YOU CAN'T UNSEE IT

*Knowing yourself is the beginning of all wisdom.*
—ARISTOTLE

Have you ever seen the FedEx logo on the side of one of their trucks as they deliver your package? Of course, you have!

But have you ever noticed that the space between the "E" and "X" is actually the shape of an arrow pointing to the right? If you've never seen it before, you're welcome—you'll never NOT see it again. Those two letters in and of themselves may seem inconsequential, but the arrow formed in between them communicates forward movement, and it grabs your attention.

That's how it is with things we can't unsee.

Let us give you another example. Imagine you're sitting at a stoplight, waiting to turn left. In front of you is a brand new, shiny black pickup truck. You know, the kind that has the tailgate big enough to see the reflection of your own car in the glassy black paint.

What you notice in that shiny tailgate while you sit there at that light is that while your turn signal is definitely on, and it's flashing on your dashboard gauge cluster, it's definitely NOT blinking on the outside. You can tell by the lack of a flashing orange light on that tailgate that you have a broken left front turn signal.

Once you see it, you can't unsee it—and now you have a decision to make.

> Once you see it, you can't unsee it.

The work of self-discovery as part of the transformational journey is much like that. Once we uncover something in us, we simply can't unsee it. And what's true about that is what we uncover and what we find has probably been waiting to be discovered for a very long time. It's likely that we're finding something or some pattern of being that has been present and has impacted us for a very long time.

Just as it's likely that your turn signal was out long before you noticed it was out in the reflection on that shiny tailgate, so it is with your patterns of behavior that are simply waiting to be seen.

So many people we encounter say some version of this statement: "What if, in the process of self-discovery, I find something I don't like?" Well, that's possible. But here's one way to think about that question using the turn signal analogy. Finding a broken turn signal is unpleasant, especially in a new car. In a new car, that could very easily mean you'll be looking at a fix that costs hundreds of dollars! But consider the alternative. The alternative is that you continue driving around with an inoperable turn signal, risking a collision at every left-hand turn. Short term, that fix is quite unpleasant. But long term, it's completely necessary.

This "once you see it, now you can't unsee it" reality can be the difference between short-term hurt and long-term harm.

Circling all the way back to the early chapters of this book, the short-term hurt of digging in to understand why we feel the need to hide our failures at work—which causes us to work that second job, leaving us exhausted, frustrated, and in a constant state of overwhelm—far outweighs the long-term harm of never changing.

Dr. Henry Cloud referenced the results of long-term harm when he wrote about the death spiral of the leader about a decade ago.[23] When our brains take in new information, and we process that information as if it is beyond our control, three opportunities are created: What we see can become personal, pervasive, and permanent.

The value of the transformational journey is in both our *ability* and *willingness* to assess the information our brains receive. By now, you have been granted a lot of tools to understand what's happening. Is this a protective promise? Is it a firefighter or a manager? Is this a "me" problem, or is this outside of me?

Once we see it, we can't unsee it, which can prevent an issue from becoming pervasive. If we see it and leave it alone, assuming we can, "it" can continue unchecked. The brain then generalizes the problem, and everything becomes more serious or pervasive, which leads to problems and patterns of behavior that become permanent.

> Is there anything keeping you from extending grace and self-compassion when you see it?

Let's pause for a moment. It's entirely possible that self-discovery could cause you to see and subsequently not be able to unsee something that is tremendously painful and maybe even capital "T" traumatic. If you were to have that experience, what we'd say to you is, "Tap the brakes."

What would it take for you to give yourself some self-compassion and grace to feel what you're feeling at a level you can handle? Is there anything keeping you from extending grace and self-compassion when you see it?

---

[23] Dr. Henry Cloud, "Reversing the Death Spiral of a Leader," Global Leadership Network, February 13, 2015, https://globalleadership.org/videos/leading-yourself/reversing-the-death-spiral-of-a-leader.

We also would like you to know that there is no shame in being where you are. Sometimes, the reality of seeing something that has been exiled as long as it has can be debilitating. It's okay. If that's you, and if you have uncovered a traumatic experience along the way, we want to gently invite you to find a really good therapist. Even those surprising or traumatic things are better uncovered and seen, but they may require a more clinical approach to reap the fruit that comes from uncovering them.

However, for instances like those of our friends all the way back in the "Introduction" that may not include experiences of "capital T" trauma, we extend the same gentle invitation to continue to uncover at a rate you can handle.

Our experience would also cause us to be so bold as to say: Engaging what you have seen when you can't unsee it is best done with a trusted guide (maybe even a Brimstone Coaching Group coach). The fruit that can be unlocked after the seeing is both beautiful and profound. We would both say that our transformational journeys occurred over time in fits and starts. We each had moments in our lives when we questioned ourselves and why we were doing the things we were doing, but it wasn't until that wise guide held up the mirror for us that we could really process our way through it.

CHAPTER

# 7

# AGENCY

*Only I can change my life. No one can do it for me.*
—CAROL BURNETT

As we compile all these thoughts, principles, and tools into what you're currently holding in your hands, it's early 2025. Astute readers will know just how polarized and divided we as a people are today. I (Kurt) can sit here at my desk, firmly located in a small town in the middle of America, and look out the window to find an SUV driving by on Highway 10 with a full-sized back window decal that proudly declares "F&*k Biden." Hardly a rallying cry for unity and neighborly bridge building.

That's not all that I can "see." Looking out my metaphorical window, I see the lasting effects of the global pandemic in 2020. I see immigrants and minorities scared for their safety and status. I see racial tensions high. I see families struggling to pay for necessities, living amidst rising inflation. That's just to name a few things.

Why do I mention this in a book about transformation and wholeness? Well, there are a couple reasons. First, these things are significant contributors to the amount of stress and anxiety we feel in our lived experience. No matter how we feel about them, whether we agree or disagree with what's happening and how these tensions are being handled, they absolutely affect our day-to-day lives. Many of us like to think that we can isolate ourselves from the impact of these things, maybe by avoiding them, but we simply cannot. These waters, waters filled with anxiety, are simply the waters we swim in.

The American Psychological Association shares some alarming statistics that show what are "significant sources of stress" for American adults today. High percentages of us feel these sources of stress:

- Inflation – 83 percent of Americans
- Violence & Crime – 75 percent of Americans
- Political Climate – 66 percent of Americans
- Racial Tensions – 62 percent of Americans[24]

And perhaps most alarming in this survey and report is that 27 percent of American adults surveyed self-reported that most days, they are so stressed that they cannot function well. Think about that. Just over one in four American adults feel a stress level that impacts how they show up in the places they live, work, and play!

I imagine that none of this really comes as a surprise to you, reader. It's likely not a question of *if* you can place yourself in those statistics but more of a question of *where* you place yourself. Chris and I lament deeply that this is true. We lament deeply the amount of brokenness and dysfunction those things bring to real people's lives, and not just in the abstract. They ARE real, and so are their consequences.

One of the most important lessons the transformational journey has afforded me (Chris) is that I do not have to be a victim of my circumstances.

That is a strong word, isn't it? Victim!

---

[24] "Stress in America 2022," American Psychological Association, https://www.apa.org/news/press/releases/stress/2022/concerned-future-inflation.

I use that word on purpose here because of my propensity to play the victim. When I play the victim, I find myself stuck in patterns of behavior that leave me feeling exhausted, frustrated, and in a state of overwhelm. When I think about the idea of having agency, I believe I actually have the capacity to influence my own behaviors and my own thoughts. When I have agency, I have taken back control over how I show up in the world.

When I think about the idea of agency through an internal family systems (IFS) lens, the true self is the one guiding my actions in a relaxed state. In a state of overwhelm, when I feel as though I am the victim, my protector parts get into gear to spare my exiled parts from feeling the things I felt when I exiled them in the first place.

Here's the thing about victimhood, for me, friends. I am not my best self, my truest self, when I blame, complain, and defend. When I play the victim, I blame, complain, and defend—totally shirking my responsibility and the part that I play in keeping situations alive that lead to brokenness and dysfunction.

This brings us to the second and most important reason to bring these things up. We simply have very little control over how these things play out. Now, don't hear me say that this should lead us to apathy because that's not the case. We believe deeply that those areas of brokenness and hurt in our communities should not only drive us to care but should also drive us to *action*.

Instead, here's what "we have very little control over these things" really means. It means I simply cannot change the mind of my neighbor who thinks so differently than me that it causes me stress. You simply cannot change the words that your one aunt uses at the Thanksgiving dinner table that make your face nearly automatically land in your palms. Or, if you remember my example earlier when I was sitting at a lunch table with my friend Luke, I couldn't make him get angry like I was (or thought I was). Completely unbothered by my unease around the government action that had me rattled, he challenged me with, "What difference does this make in your daily life?" As much as we'd like to change those things and those people, we just cannot. And just maybe, that's not the change that's most needed!

Maybe the change that's actually needed most is a change in the way we respond to those situations. In fact, this is *exactly* the change that's needed, and it's the only change that we can possibly influence.

This is really helpful to understand. I believe Murray Bowen and other experts in family systems theory would say that the highest point of leverage for change in any organization, system, or situation is the way we show up in it.

> The highest point of leverage for change in any organization, system, or situation is the way we show up in it.

Having agency means we take responsibility for ourselves and the way we "be" in these places and spaces. When someone sees the world of politics differently than I do, I can allow my protective promise to be poked or pressed, and I will respond in some rather predictable ways. When this happens, I blame them for making me feel certain ways and don't take responsibility for lashing out.

"You're the one . . ."

Have you ever said those words in an argument? "You're the one who said that about them. And when you say things about them, I get mad, and I retaliate." While it may be true that someone says something that gets me stirred up—or even mad—the other person is not responsible for my actions, behaviors, outbursts, or shame. I am! I am responsible, and because I am and because I have agency, this transformational journey is vital!

Have you ever left social media or the news feeling stirred up, unsure why you're so stirred? Yeah, us too. And here's one thing we know: Social media and news, and the people that cause us to get stirred up, aren't going away. Those things aren't concerned that we get stirred up by their behavior or comments. And it's getting harder and harder to completely disconnect from social media. So, if those things aren't going to change, and if we can't change them, we invite you to address your own reaction.

Your metaphorical aunt at Thanksgiving (or maybe not so metaphorical) will continue to make comments that trigger you. Do you want those comments to control your day and negatively impact your Thanksgiving experience with the rest of your family? Of course, you don't. And we're here to tell you that you have agency to do the transformational work to change those outcomes, EVEN IF your aunt never does change.

Or what about our friend Lucy from the Introduction, who was stopped and stuck for some time by what her family of origin might think of her life and her parenting. Rather than trying to figure out how to get her family to think differently about her parenting (in vain, of course), she did the hard work in herself to unlock her transformation so that she could get unstuck *independent of* her family.

You CAN do this work! You CAN affect transformation in your life!

But there's a challenging word in here too. "You CAN do the work" feels pretty encouraging, but maybe the next phrase might not feel as encouraging. ONLY you can do the work!

**ONLY you can do the work!**

For what it's worth, I (Kurt) would very much like someone else to do this work of transformation for me, at least in part. But it just doesn't work like that for me, and it doesn't work like that for you. So this is where we invite you to make a decision now that you have seen all you've seen in your life with the help of the tools in these pages. Are you going to lean in and take the first step on the transformational journey? Will you take responsibility for your own growth?

We very much hope that you will!

CHAPTER

# 8

# WHY THE TRANSFORMATIONAL JOURNEY MATTERS

*We can pretend that we have nothing to learn, or we can take this opportunity to own the truth and make a better future for ourselves and others.*
—BRENÉ BROWN

Given all that we've covered, we thought it would be helpful to provide you with some everyday reasons to engage in the transformational journey. All the places and spaces we find ourselves benefit from our continued work to become the truest, most whole version of ourselves that we can be.

The sections of this chapter are some of the best and most effective ways to put the theory of this book into practice, as well as how to contextualize the learning in tangible leadership scenarios.

## BREAKING THROUGH SELF-DOUBT IN LEADERSHIP

Leading is hard! Period. Maybe you lead in a corporate space. Maybe you lead a team of people and projects, moving them toward a shared strategic goal. Maybe you lead on an athletic field as a player or coach. Maybe you lead your family through every single day in your home, cheering on kids as they grow and mature. Hear us say again: ALL leadership is hard, and ALL leadership requires you to show up as your whole self!

Because leadership is so hard, it's likely you sometimes feel stuck. Sometimes, it feels like you're bumping up against a glass ceiling of sorts keeping you from your full potential. Sometimes, it feels like there's something keeping you from contentment in your work and leadership, the fulfillment you hope your success will bring, or the wholeness you so desperately desire in your home. Sometimes, you feel exhausted because you are not content in your work and leadership.

While there might be any number of contributing factors to a ceiling like this, we believe that one major factor is self-doubt.

The potential for self-doubt lies around every corner of life. Maybe you've heard this sort of self-doubt called "Imposter Syndrome." It's pervasive today! And it manifests in internal questions like:

- What if my colleagues realize I don't belong?
- What if I don't deserve the position or role that I'm in?
- What if I'm found out by my superiors?
- What if I can't perform when I need to perform?

This is not only pervasive, it's exhausting—we know! Why? Because we have done that dance and lived that life.

But what if you didn't have to do that dance anymore? What if you didn't have to worry about being found out? What if there wasn't actually anything to be found out?

At Brimstone Coaching Group, we believe deeply that each of us shows up to lead doing two jobs. First, we do the job and the leading that's actually ours to do, whether it's in our family or in a paid or volunteer position. The second job is the job of hiding or the job of keeping people from "finding out."

You don't need us to tell you that this second job is not only far more exhausting and demanding than your first job but it also keeps you from leading most fully and authentically. The self-doubt it sows in you keeps your true self from showing up!

As the wise philosopher Ron Swanson once said, "Never half-ass two things, whole-ass one thing!"

## THE POWER OF SELF-DISCOVERY

So what's the solution to self-doubt and our working the second job of hiding while trying to lead? Just stop it, right? Well, no. We don't think it's that simplistic. We actually don't think the answer is ever "try harder." Like you, if the answer was "try harder," we'd have already stopped working that second job!

Instead, we ask you to consider that there is actually something keeping you stuck and keeping you from doing the things you've always done in response to feeling like an imposter. And it's self-discovery that will unlock the answers inside you.

It's something internal! Again, while external factors certainly contribute, we believe it's most fruitful to begin looking inside and learning to manage and navigate the internal factors that contribute to self-doubt because those are the only factors we can begin to take steps toward transforming.

The way forward is to go back. No, that's not a joke, nor is it simply a cliché!

Remember the protective promises you began uncovering and unlocking in Chapter Four? We really believe that self-doubt and "Imposter Syndrome" are firmly rooted in something that you experienced in the past, likely in a pattern of behavior that your protective promise helped you create.

Think about it. If you stop and ponder this feeling of self-doubt or the feeling of being an imposter, we think you'll probably be able to trace it back (maybe slowly over time) to an experience where someone told you (implicitly or explicitly) that you don't belong or that you aren't good enough to do what you're doing.

When I (Kurt) was in the third grade, I participated in the third-grade spelling bee. Before you get too excited, it was a small elementary school in Illinois, so it wasn't exactly the National Scripps Spelling Bee.

But I was a really good speller! Actually, I was a good memorizer! And I breezed through the first few rounds, up until there were only three of us competitors left. My turn came up, and in front of the whole elementary school student body, teachers, staff, and parents, the moderator said: "Your word is 'farm.'" Easy peasy, right? That's what I thought too! But out of my little third-grade mouth came this: "Farm. F-R-A-M. Farm." You can see the problem. The moderator rang the little bell, and that was the end of my championship run!

That was the beginning of the voice in me that would say, "You know you're going to mess this up again." It didn't matter what it was, "You know you're going to mess this up again" was all too ready to jump in and keep me safe from the embarrassment I felt when I said "F-R-A-M."

You probably didn't misspell "farm" in the third-grade spelling bee, but you probably had some experience that continues to feed the belief that you don't belong. If you have not yet, go back to Chapter Four and spend some time getting clear on potential protective promises that might be keeping you stuck.

$$E + R = T$$
*encounters + reflection = transformation*

Times like that, when you feel self-doubt, are the perfect times to work the Transformational Equation (E+R=T). Those times are encounters, and when you notice them, see if you can take a breath. Stop for a little bit, even if it's just a couple of minutes, and reflect on what's going on in you. Reflect on how you feel. Maybe write those things down, jot down a note in your phone, or create a voice memo for later. And while you may not be able to do any of that in the moment, put a mental "pin" in what's going on and come back to the "R" a little later.

Don't rush past the encounters of self-doubt, and don't skip reflection. As Kurt might say, when we ask, "What's true?" in those scenarios, it's rarely true that you're an imposter. It's rarely true that you don't belong. What IS true is that you can begin to put those feelings behind you.

And maybe just to be clear one more time, this is not just theory! We believe that the fruits of this transformational journey are real and will have real implications and impact on your daily experience of life.

One of the things that we see as coaches is that there are some experiences that are nearly unanimously experienced by all humans. These are things like overwhelm, uncertainty of how to navigate conflict and anger, and dealing with a loud inner self-critic, just to name a few.

So we're going to give you some practical application for these very relatable experiences in this chapter. And while we get to see that these are commonly felt experiences, it's likely that you, the reader, feel you might be the only human feeling them. That maybe there is something wrong with you. That maybe you just don't have it figured out as well as the next person. Well, know that you are not alone. There is nothing wrong with you. And nobody really has it (whatever "it" is) figured out. We're all just doing the best we can. So, at the very least, may the rest of this chapter remind you that you're in good company!

## BREAKING FREE FROM OVERWHELM: FINDING BALANCE WHEN LIFE FEELS TOO DEMANDING

Today, the twin feelings of overwhelm and overcommitment are ubiquitous. These are simply the waters we swim in, and often, the fullness of our calendars and the busyness of our lives can leave us with these twin sinking feelings. What's more worrisome is that there are times we can see the fullness of our calendar and the busyness of our lives almost like a badge of honor. Many of us are simply doing whatever we can to keep our heads above water, to little or no avail. Consider these alarming statistics:

- More than 75 percent of Americans report symptoms of stress that include headaches, tiredness, and depression.
- 83 percent of American employees report work-related stress.
- And maybe most alarming, nearly half (49 percent) of American adults report that stress has negatively impacted their behavior.[25]

> Living from your truest self is the antidote to overwhelm and exhaustion.

I wonder if you are part of those statistics. Would you put yourself in one of those categories? If so, we want you to hear us say that you don't have to be one of those statistics any longer. The result of being one of these statistics is often feeling exhausted, frustrated, and overloaded because you are in a state of overwhelm. Living from your truest self is the antidote to overwhelm and exhaustion, and as we've been showing throughout the previous pages, you can, in fact, begin the transformational journey to live as your truest self today! It doesn't matter whether you're twenty years old or ninety years old—transformation is possible.

How, you ask? Well, first, we have to understand why we feel overwhelmed.

To be sure, there are a number of factors that contribute to overwhelm and the reality of being overcommitted. Some of them are external factors like:

- Your company just downsized, and now you're wearing two hats at work instead of your normal single hat.
- You have a growing family, and your kids simply need to be in different places all at the same time, seemingly every night of the week.

---

[25] "Stress in America 2022," APA.

- Unexpected life changes or challenges happen, forcing you to adjust to a new reality without warning.

Maybe you noticed that those external factors are all largely outside of your control. You don't get a say in them. And often, you can't change them easily or at all. These happen. No matter how in control we feel, ultimately, control of our lives is an illusion. Sometimes, the proverbial monkey wrench gets thrown into our lives.

However, there are also internal factors that contribute to overwhelm, and the good news is that you CAN impact those and change them over time with the help of the Transformational Equation and replacing protective promises with purposeful and preferred promises.

The challenge in all of this is that even in those times when life is overly busy and challenging, or when life changes are thrust upon you, you are STILL working the second job of hiding. That pattern of behavior that came from your protective promise doesn't just stop because you have to add a "hat" at work to compensate for coworkers who were laid off. It's entirely possible that you might work harder and more diligently at that second job of hiding when life gets busy and you start to feel overwhelmed. You start grasping for control.

Think about that . . .

While you're:

- Leading your team through a strategic planning session that NEEDS to be done today.
- Preparing that presentation that's due Monday.
- Teaching your child long division for the first time while also trying to refresh your own learning.
- Volunteering at your favorite nonprofit organization.
- Flying across town in your minivan to drop kids off at practices.

While you're doing all these things, you're also hiding parts of yourself in order to feel safe and protected and constantly wondering, "Am I doing enough?" Or maybe you're even wondering how you could possibly slow down without those around you thinking less of you.

Sounds exhausting, doesn't it? That's because it IS exhausting!

And we believe it's true that we ALL do this nearly every day thanks to those protective promises we created all those years ago.

As an adult, it might go like this:

- While you're leading your team, you find yourself consumed by the fear that your team will begin to think you're a bad leader.
- While you're preparing the presentation that's due Monday, you find yourself most motivated by the fear of embarrassment during the presentation itself.
- You find yourself unexpectedly escalating and ramping up emotionally while teaching your child long division because you know the neighbor kid can already do it better.
- You snap at your child in the back seat of the van because you've stretched your time margins too thin in this moment.

Thanks to your long-held protective promises, those patterns of behavior that keep you stuck running around at breakneck speed are just normal.

As we asked earlier in the chapter, doesn't every adult feel this way?

Maybe. The stats have shown that most adults do actually feel this way. But does that make this way of adulting beneficial or good? We would say no—no, it doesn't. I (Kurt) have my mother's voice rattling in my head while I write this: "If your friend jumped off a bridge, would you too?" Point taken, Mom. Probably not.

What if we told you that there's another way to "adult"? What if there is a way that's more intentional, more purposeful, and, most importantly, more sustainable?

For starters, we want to offer you some real and tangible practices that might function as counter-systems to the systems that keep you in a state of overwhelm:

- **Get some rest** – Physically AND emotionally. Find some time in your rhythm to slow down and take a breath, even for just a minute or two. Go to bed thirty minutes early a couple nights a week. Instead of turning on Netflix or going to social media in downtime, sit in a comfortable chair and read a book, draw a picture, journal, or just listen to the wind rustle some leaves.
- **Find time to be unhurried** – Turn the podcast off in your car on the way home from work. Do the speed limit on the way home from work instead of going ten over so you can process your day. Take five minutes of your lunch hour and be alone, just to take some deep breaths. Listen to your body. Carve out time before you go to sleep to reflect back on the last twenty-four hours and how you showed up in them.
- **Do something that brings you joy** – Do that thing or that hobby that you know you love to do but haven't been making time for. Put a puzzle together, hop on that bicycle, weed your garden, or go for a long, quiet walk. Volunteer for a nonprofit organization you really love. It's OK to make time for something you love to do!
- **Engage your whole self** – If you work primarily with your hands and physical body, engage your mind by reading a book, journaling, or listening to a podcast that makes you think and reflect. If you work primarily with your mind, engage your physical body by mowing your yard, organizing a closet, or cleaning out your car.

There is great freedom and great momentum to be gained in taking even *one small step* out of the rhythm of overwhelm, reflecting on what actually is as you pursue contentment, fulfillment, and wholeness.

But let's all just be honest with

one another—while these practices are great, they also need to be approached with discipline and integrity. If you typically end your night with an hour of scrolling social media, you will not naturally just give that up one day. It will take work. Make a preferred promise to yourself. Tell a friend which of those practices you're going to try on. Be intentional and hold yourself to it!

## INCORPORATING BOUNDARIES TO AVOID OVERWHELM

There's one more thing that will help you take significant steps toward living a life free from overwhelm, and that's the ability to set good boundaries.

What are boundaries? I (Kurt) always held the mental model that a boundary was a metaphorical brick wall governed by a flowchart. When faced with a chance to take something on or to overcommit, I'd run that situation through a metaphorical internal flowchart populated with yes/no questions based on what I have said I will do and won't do. So when something popped up in front of me that needed a decision, I inserted the question into the metaphorical flowchart and let it do its thing. Flowcharts always work flawlessly, right?

Right—until the nuances of the gray areas of life pop up. The reality is most of life is gray and doesn't fit into the neat and tidy flowchart of yes/no questions like I wanted it to.

So, instead of a brick wall, I wonder what would happen if you imagined a boundary being a drawbridge. What if that drawbridge enabled you to make decisions based on your best thinking, principles, and values? It's a drawbridge, not a brick wall, which allows you to make decisions about your time and energy that reflect what you're responsible for and what is sustainable in keeping your head above water.

This is a key to come out of the cycles of overwhelm and overcommitment. Understanding the protective promises younger you made in order to feel safe and not overwhelmed. Creating healthy boundaries to enable you to limit your commitments in healthy ways leads to experiencing the feeling of safety in your life that overwhelm and overcommitment have robbed you of.

Once you get on top of the water, if you will, rather than fighting to keep your head above water, being willing to ask and answer these questions will enable you to stay on top of the water:

- Can I actually control what others think of me?
- Does overcommitting actually do what I think it will do in people's perception of me?
- Do I need to try to take on the burden of guessing what my coworkers will think of me while I'm doing the best work I can do?
- Do I need to take responsibility for my coworkers and their stress by overstretching my capacity to help them with their workload?

It's on top of the water that we have been able to ask and answer these questions for ourselves. As it was when we were younger humans, people who already knew how to swim taught us how to swim too. They kept us from drowning, taught us how to keep our heads above water, and finally showed us how to thrive on top of the water.

This is how we learned to deal with overwhelm and overcommitment too. The wise guides we've mentioned a couple of times have come alongside us, helped us experience the feeling of safety once again, and taught us how to create clear boundaries.

Lastly, at the risk of sounding like a broken record, we invite you to work the Transformational Equation (E+R=T) when you feel most overwhelmed. It will likely feel counterintuitive and counterproductive to stop and reflect, but this is really where transformation lies. Doing nothing in those moments will only lead to more overwhelm.

## MANAGING CONFLICT WITH COMPASSION: RESPONDING TO ANGER AND FRUSTRATION WITH PURPOSE

I (Chris) remember it like it was yesterday. The members of the board and I gathered around the table to listen to the presentation the consultant (one we collectively hired) had put together based on how we assessed ourselves organizationally.

As a system, we were stuck, and everyone knew it. While our frustrations varied, and the way we saw ourselves in the system did, too, we agreed before even beginning the consultant's assessment that we would listen intently to the report and proceed with his recommendations once we had them.

Until we had them!

That's when everything went south, or so I thought for a long time.

When the consultant presented his findings and mapped a path forward for our consideration and organizational flourishing, the board president quickly quashed the entire report, dismissed the recommendations, and, along with it, any hope of organizational transformation.

I was instantly angry. Fuming. Ready to fight. Spitting nails. Virtually any and every other metaphor that comes to your mind right now, I was feeling it. In the moment, I pushed back and tried to hold up a mirror for the president and the rest of the board—to no avail.

The meeting ended. The president was the first to leave. There was a little of the "meeting after the meeting"—you know, where we talked behind his back and not to his face—but because I was seeing red, I couldn't really engage in those conversations.

Truth is, I didn't really engage the rest of the regular meeting. I was so angry and frustrated with what had transpired that I couldn't stop thinking about it. In fact, I took it home with me. I was not present with my wife and kids that evening, and I woke even more angry the next morning.

Remember how I told you that everything went south once we had the consultant's recommendations? I have come to understand differently.

For much of my life, I believed that other people were the problem. I believed their actions, their thoughts, and their words were the problem. What I have come to learn later in life is this: The problem is rarely "out there"—the problem is "in here." And when I say in here, all ten fingers are pointing directly at me. And let's be clear: By "problem," I mean the issue to be addressed or the issue at hand.

I wonder if you can relate. Have you ever believed that the problem was "out there"?

This is what I have come to understand over time. The only thing I can control in any circumstance, relationship, or situation is me—my emotions, my feelings, the meaning I make, and the reactions I have to those circumstances, relationships, and situations.

That's it!

The president of the board wasn't the problem. Nor was the inactivity of the rest of the board. The problem, really, was the fact that my anger and frustration took control of me, and I could not behave in ways that were true to who I am as a leader or in ways that helped the organization move forward.

As it turns out, I was the problem. My reactivity led me into overwhelm, and, like most humans, I did things I learned to do in my formational years to return to a feeling of being safe. And, you guessed it, my protective promise caused all sorts of autopilot patterns of behavior to happen in me. That automatic response took control of my ability to respond even before I knew it was happening.

I imagine you've had a similar experience in the places you live, work, or play. You've likely seen red the way I saw red—the type of red that makes everything else invisible.

## HOPE LIES IN HOW WE SHOW UP

There is hope! What we have learned is the highest point of leverage for change in any situation is the way we show up in the situation. What that means is as we deeply desire our systems and spaces to experience transformation, the work we do in ourselves around transformation is the most effective way to bring change. Seems counterintuitive, doesn't it?

Hope is found in the fact that we can create more intentional and preferred promises, the same preferred promises we spent time establishing in Chapter Four.

Remember, preferred promises enable us to prepare in advance for meetings we have scheduled, that family reunion that we don't want to attend, or any situation we can think of where we have not responded or shown up the way we would want to in the past.

Preferred promises give us agency and enable us to respond in ways that are rooted in our best thinking. Understanding my protective promises enables me to feel my autopilot kick in and subsequently make a decision: Do I want to allow my anger and frustration to be the feelings driving my response here, or would I prefer to behave differently?

Because I left so many meetings and other situations where "I will not be controlled" was my response, regret and remorse created the low hum with which I lived my life. My preferred promise, however, has enabled me to have compassion for myself and others in contentious situations. You can too.

If you struggle with feelings of anger and frustration, there is a way forward.

While I cannot go back and use a mulligan in that board meeting all those years ago, I have been able to manage myself in similar situations by preparing in advance, considering how I'd like to show up, and drafting preferred promises. By doing so, I'm able to navigate conflict and change in more thoughtful ways in the meetings and relationships I find myself in.

> If you struggle with feelings of anger and frustration, there is a way forward.

You can too!

## SILENCING THE INNER CRITIC: BUILDING A MINDSET OF SELF-COMPASSION AND RESILIENCE

Jim is a gifted engineer and innovation officer with a major corporation in the upper Midwest of the United States. During one of our sessions, Jim began to notice his inner critic.

He leads projects and innovates on a daily basis. Jim is also a husband, father, and leader in his community. He and his spouse have successfully raised three children and launched them out of the house and into the world as relatively well-adjusted members of society.

From the outside looking in, Jim appears to have it all.

Alas, that is not the case. Sure, there are parts of Jim that are thriving, but there are other parts of Jim that are exhausted, frustrated, and overloaded with the demands of his life. There are parts of Jim that are keeping him stuck and stopped from experiencing contentment, fulfillment, and wholeness in all the places and spaces he finds himself.

A sub-par performance review gets Jim's attention. When his supervisor highlighted the fact that systems and structures in the organization where Jim is leading aren't producing like they usually do, alarm systems begin to fire in Jim's inner being.

Am I a failure? Am I just an imposter? Is all of this finally catching up with me?

Jim's inner critic is running roughshod over the good parts of Jim, those parts that are efficient, productive, happy, content, and fulfilled as he toggles between work and family life.

Not only has the inner critic hijacked Jim's ability to innovate, feelings he experiences from the inner critic's messaging begin to impact all areas of his life. Whereas he loved to get up, make the commute to work, and lead his team during the day, he would rather stay home and do nothing.

Jim is not alone.

Chances are you have experienced similar feelings.

Everyone has an inner critic, a part of us that was wounded during our early years, first formation. That part experienced deep hurt, pain, shame, or any other number of negative emotions. Unconsciously, those parts of us were exiled deep into our psyche so that we could avoid the pain they caused.

We think about it this way: We all have experiences and make meaning from those experiences. Because these meanings are made unconsciously, they may be correct, or they may be incorrect, but meaning is made just the same.

The meaning we make informs what happens next.

Through a series of one-on-one coaching sessions, Jim came to discover that his inner critic reared its ugly head and stifled his ability to seek advancement and enjoy success. Jim said, "Though successful, I didn't feel like I deserved success. While I thought I was emotionally well, I realized a mental barrier was present and impacting my ability to truly enjoy the blessings in my life."

Discovering his protective promise, Jim was able to embrace self-compassion and become more resilient as a leader.

We talked about each encounter and the thoughts and feelings that were alive in him that day. There were others, but these were the ones that occupied most of our time. I then invited Jim to think about the one encounter where he felt stuck and stopped. That encounter happened to be the morning interactions with his team members.

It was during this conversation that Jim started to get clear on his feeling of not deserving success. We hung out here for a while, getting curious about other times that Jim experienced these feelings. He was given some homework to trace back to other times that he experienced these feelings and was invited to trace back as far as he could.

Eventually, Jim discovered that he had created a protective promise in his teenage years that he would take a backseat to others. The protective promise was, "I am not valuable."

As Jim grew up, transitioned to college, and eventually got a job, was married, and started a family, he carried that inner critic with him. While not front of mind, "I am not valuable" and the predictable behaviors that accompanied it would come out.

Not to sound like a broken record, but transformation is usually slow and happens over time. As he began to process more and more of his encounters, reflecting on them and the impact that "I am not valuable" was having on him, the transformational journey began.

## THE SECRET SAUCE OF SELF-COMPASSION

Jim was able to discover that when he was stuck and stopped by this protective promise, he became critical of himself. As I like to say, Jim would "should on himself" in front of others. "I'm sorry, I 'should' know better." Or "I know I'm holding back from sharing my thoughts with the team, and I 'shouldn't' do that."

As Jim was able to get clearer on his protective promise, he was able to begin exercising self-compassion. While not practiced well by most twenty-first-century North Americans, the idea of self-compassion is transformational.

In an article published in the *Harvard Business Review* entitled, "Give Yourself a Break: The Power of Self-Compassion," Serena Chen explains that self-compassion is a useful tool for enhancing performance in a wide range of settings, including the business world. In fact, Chen explains that self-compassion creates a sense of self-worth that leads to people genuinely caring about their own well-being and recovery from setbacks that happen in the workplace. Chen and her colleagues find these qualities in individuals with high levels of self-compassion:

- kind instead of judgmental about their own mistakes
- able to grasp that failures are a shared human experience

- ready to allow themselves to feel bad about their failures without allowing negative emotions to win the day[26]

Said another way, people who exercise self-compassion are able to be more kind to themselves, able to deal with their protective promises in healthy ways, and struggle less with shame.

For many, protective promises lead to shame. And not to be confused with guilt (that says, "I've done something bad"), shame says, "I am bad."

Being able to exercise self-compassion is an antidote to shame and allows both individuals and the organizations they work for to improve. According to Chen, "When people treat themselves with compassion, they are better able to arrive at realistic self-appraisals, which is the foundation for improvement. They are motivated to work on their weaknesses rather than think, 'What's the point?' and to summon the grit required to enhance skills and change bad habits."[27]

Slowly, and over time, Jim was able to move from the protective promise that said, "I am not valuable," to a place of self-compassion. And from that place of self-compassion, he could begin to think with purpose about what was actually true of him. He was able to create a purposeful promise so he could replace that old, worn-out protective promise.

He said, "I wanted to enjoy blessings without guilt or second-guessing." Jim replaced "I am not valuable" with the purposeful promise that says, "I am valued for who I am and what I bring to the table."

During our one-on-one sessions, I began to invite Jim to try on that more purposeful promise in the places and spaces he found himself. As he interacted with his teammates at work, his spouse, his adult children, and over lunch, when Jim began to feel those old feelings, he began to draw on his purposeful promise.

---

[26] Serena Chen, "Give Yourself a Break: The Power of Self-Compassion," *Harvard Business Review*, September–October 2018, https://hbr.org/2018/09/give-yourself-a-break-the-power-of-self-compassion.

[27] Chen, "Give Yourself."

We know how counterintuitive this all sounds, extending self-compassion to ourselves. But this transformational journey and the process of establishing new promises is one that must include a healthy and consistent dose of self-compassion. The process works. It works for Jim, it's worked for us, and it can work for you too!

## NAVIGATING CHANGE WITH CONFIDENCE: FOSTERING ADAPTABILITY IN A CULTURE OF UNCERTAINTY

In the spring of 1999, we purchased a business and relocated to a new community. We did so with a home we couldn't sell and, therefore, purchased a hundred-year-old home that had been added onto several times.

I (Chris) am not too proud to say that we lived in some rather modest accommodations early in our married years, but this home takes the cake. The home had been added onto multiple times and had two major problems.

The first issue was I would wake night after night to the sound of bats clawing around in the plaster laths. No harm, no foul for several years until they began to find their way out of the walls and into the house. The second issue was whenever a strong directional rain would take place, our roof leaked, resulting in fighting water in the laundry room that damaged both the floor and the drywall in the room.

You may be wondering, what do these things have to do with navigating change with confidence? If you're asking yourself that question, it's a fair question—thanks for asking it. There is a difference between technical problems and adaptive challenges. If you are a CEO, a team lead, or an employee in an organization trying to navigate change, you know this is true.

Technical problems are usually situations that can be solved by an expert or by using information you already have at your disposal. Usually, technical problems are easy to identify, are solved relatively quickly, and suggested solutions are readily approved.

Adaptive challenges, on the other hand, are situations that are harder to identify; the solution isn't readily available. They require a systematic approach to resolve and necessitate change in numerous places. Adaptive challenges also require solutions that are not very popular.

| Technical Problems | Adaptive Challenges |
|---|---|
| • Easy to identify | • Hard to identify |
| • Solvable by an expert or currently held knowledge | • Solutions are not readily available |
| • Suggested Solutions are welcome | • Suggested solutions are met with resistance |

At first blush, our home issues produced technical problems, particularly when I think about the roof issue. Replace a shingle here and there; perhaps install a new piece of flashing, and the problem would be resolved.

False. The adaptive challenge that was necessary was to change the slope of the roof. And pertaining to the bat issue, let's just say the only real solution was to burn the entire place to the ground and start over.

Instead of working through all the adaptive challenges staring us in the face, we built a new house on the south side of town, away from the bat-infested part of the community and did so with a reputable builder to avoid water and bat issues.

If I knew then what I know now, I may have handled the housing situation differently. I did not have the resources at my disposal to know the differences between technical problems and adaptive challenges, nor did I understand why I was so threatened by the situation. What I didn't know that I didn't know forced our familial hand. And what's also true about all of this is that what I didn't know that I didn't know was showing up in other areas of my life.

So it is with leaders. You are confronted with dozens of situations every day. Opportunities present themselves for you to lead your organization and your team to unprecedented heights, but those things that you don't yet know and the threats that accompany those things keep you stuck and the organization prevented from becoming all it can be.

## FOSTERING ADAPTABILITY BEGINS WITH YOU

At the Brimstone Coaching Group, we often say to our clients that we believe deeply in the idea that fostering adaptability in a culture of uncertainty is crucial to organizational health. Understanding that your system is getting exactly the results it is designed to get is a good place to start, and, as the leader, it begins with you.

As the leader, you will always be the lid on top of the organization. If you desire the organization you lead to adapt and grow with the times, YOU must adapt and grow with the times. If you desire your team to innovate in a season of uncertainty, YOU must allow them to both fail and succeed.

This is no easy task. You can't run away from it and go build a new house. Changing the slope of the roof isn't the answer either. Rather, the highest point of leverage for change in any system is the way YOU show up in it.

Ronald Heifetz, the father of adaptive leadership, would agree. Heifetz realized that our brains play an integral role in training our bodies to become proficient at new techniques of diagnosis and action. "Your whole self constitutes a resource for exercising leadership." In his book *The Practice of Adaptive Leadership*, he explained this notion as the convergence of multiple intelligences—our minds, our hearts, and our bodies.

Heifetz notes:

"One distinctive aspect of leading adaptive change is that you must connect with the values, beliefs, and anxieties of the people you are trying to move. Acts of leadership not only require you to access all parts of yourself... but to be successful, you also need to fully engage people with all these parts of yourself as well."[28]

But what if there was something keeping you from fully accessing what Heifetz calls "all parts of yourself"? What if you aren't able to engage fully with others using all those parts? If that's true, then you've found the root of what is currently keeping you as the limiting factor ("lid") in the growth and health of your organization or family and what might unlock the necessary adaptive work to raise the lid, if you will.

You guessed it, it's your protective promises showing up again! There isn't a doubt in either of our minds that the thing that keeps us stuck where we are—as it pertains to our adaptive leadership—is the degree to which we've named and addressed our protective promises.

Lucky for us, we can unlearn those old ways of being that came with our protective promises in favor of new ways of being.

Twenty-first-century neuroscience helps us understand that the brain stores information and the body keeps the score.[29] In fact, when we have experiences that trigger our protective promises, we often feel it and get into action before the brain even detects what's happening.

> We can unlearn those old ways of being that came with our protective promises in favor of new ways of being.

When our community experienced record flooding last year, and our building was decimated by floodwaters, the feelings that came rushing to the surface were the same as when I had experiences when I was fourteen and six years old. Thankfully, my response as a leader this summer was more purposeful. The result of the

---

[28] Ronald A. Heifetz, Marty Linsky, and Alexander Grashow, *The Practice of Adaptive Leadership: Tools and Tactics for Changing Your Organization and the World* (Boston: Harvard Business Review Press, 2009), 38.

[29] Eagleman, *Livewired*, 7.

LIVE FULLY LEAD AUTHENTICALLY

transformational journey for me resulted, over time, in a more purposeful promise that says, "It's okay, and I'm okay."

The same can be said for the experience of having a direct report come in three days after walking into that flooded building, telling me she was resigning. Her resignation came on the heels of another resignation just before the flood—and "I will not be controlled" and everything that accompanies it was ready to get to work.

Instead, I was able to see these situations for the adaptive challenges they were and continue to lead through uncertainty in ways that are true to who I am and how I want to be as a leader. What I'd always done was not going to work in handling these new, unexpected leadership challenges.

As these pages are being written in 2025, the need for strong, adaptive leadership seems more important than ever. Between political polarization, continued racial tensions in our communities, and the ever-present reality of ballooning inflation (among many other challenges), we will continue to see MORE adaptive challenges and fewer technical challenges.

It's as important as ever to take time to go back to Chapter Four, if you haven't already, and put real, intentional effort into creating and establishing purposeful and preferred promises in order to access "all parts of yourself," as Heifetz says while responding to more and more challenging adaptive problems.

Fostering adaptability in a culture of uncertainty begins with you, the leader. Your organization NEEDS you to do this work. Not only that, but the world also NEEDS you to do this work! Start the work today—begin the process of transformation by leaning into self-discovery and bring your team with you as you do so. Transformation like this is vital to the health and success of any organization in 2025!

> Your organization NEEDS you to do this work. The world also NEEDS you to do this work!

## QUIETING OVERTHINKING: STRATEGIES FOR CLEAR DECISION-MAKING

We've all been there. You have an important email that needs to go out. Maybe you need to communicate:

- A proposed change to a system or process.
- An explanation as to why something happened, or didn't happen, contrary to the plans.
- For the first time with a new coworker that you really want to make a good impression with.

Or maybe you have to communicate something outside of a traditional work setting:

- Messages to your kid's teacher
- Feedback to the board members of that nonprofit you love

Whatever it is, we've all been there.
But where is "there" really?
It's that moment after you've thoughtfully and intentionally crafted the words and contents of the message that needs to be sent. After you've proofread the message to make sure you haven't used "your" when you actually mean "you're." After you've added that comma you missed the first time around. After you deem the message "good to go"!
"There" is the moment that happens as you hover the cursor over the send button, when something stops you. An invisible force keeps your right index finger from landing on that left mouse button, leaving that message in the "draft" folder.
That's when the doubting begins.

- Was my tone nice enough?
- Will the recipient think I'm being rude or too direct?

- Did I sound smart enough?
- Will the recipient laugh when they read it or think my writing is terrible?
- What might that exclamation point communicate? Should I change it to a period?

We've all been there. "There" has a name: it's called analysis paralysis. Or, more simply put, let's call it overthinking.

As I (Kurt) write this, I realize I felt this literally just the other day. I typed up a text to a person I really wanted to enter into a business relationship with. After I typed the text, I proofread it, but my thumb just would not get any closer to the "send" arrow than a hover. I was stuck. I got lost in questions like:

- Was I too forward?
- Will my choice of words make me sound competent enough?
- Will an exclamation point convey that I'm overly excited?

The analysis paralysis was real!

But there's something glaring missing in questions I was asking myself as I was unable to send my text message, I wonder if you caught it. I wasn't asking:

- Is my message conveying what I want/need to communicate?
- Are the words true?
- Is the message coming from my truest self, meaning it's come from my best thinking?

Had I asked those questions instead, there would have been an easy answer. Yes! A resounding "yes"! Instead, I got stuck in analysis paralysis. Analysis paralysis happens when we get lost in asking questions to which we have no way of knowing the answers. I have no way of truly knowing what another human will feel or think when they receive my message.

What's also true is that analysis paralysis even has a greater impact beyond the ways we communicate. It also deeply impacts the way we make decisions. We hear so many stories of leaders who put in all the really hard work to get to the point of making a crucial decision for their family, their organization, or their team, only to stop short of actually making the decision out of fear or worry about others' responses to the decision.

Take Stephanie, for example. Stephanie spent months putting in the work to understand her staff and the factors that led to deep team dysfunction and isolation. And Stephanie, in her best thinking, resolved to shake up her staff and make some pretty hard but necessary changes.

But as the time came to make the decision and begin implementing her plan, she pulled up. She got stuck and paralyzed by the question, "What will other staff and my peers think of my leadership?" and "What will I do with people who disagree with me?" Or perhaps the most paralyzing question of all: "If I'm wrong, does that make me a bad leader?"

> Overthinking and succumbing to analysis paralysis does not make you a bad leader. It simply means that you are human.

Stephanie's best thinking was hijacked by overthinking.

Reader, allow me to give this truth to you very clearly: Overthinking and succumbing to analysis paralysis does not make you a bad leader. It didn't make Stephanie a bad leader. It simply means that you are human.

Here's another truth: Your family, your team, and your organization NEED you to get unstuck and begin to set aside overthinking. What's more, is that the world needs your best thinking and your whole self. Not your stuck self.

And there is good news—there are steps you can take and tools you can build to make fruitful progress toward a way of being that includes less and less analysis paralysis and overthinking.

We'll get there, but in order to go forward, we must first look back. Back once again to protective promises, because it's those promises that are driving the bus of analysis paralysis. Those promises make all of those questions and threats and fears feel all to present right here, right now.

They all FEEL so real even today, don't they? Yes, very much so! It feels like:

- You are one bad email from your peers rejecting you.
- Your whole family is judging your every parenting move.
- Your direct reports are laughing at you.

But what if they're not real? Or, more to the point, what if you didn't have to guard against those things any longer? How would you feel?

Does it feel like freedom from overthinking? Yes, I think so too!

But, dear reader, allow us to say to you one more time, with all the compassion and gentleness we can muster: Freedom is waiting for you, but it only comes once those old, protective promises are replaced (little by little each day) with your purposeful promises. We wish there was an "easy button" to push that would allow us and you to skip the hard work of establishing new promises, but there simply is no such button.

As we've said, it's difficult work, but it's worthwhile, and you can do it!

CHAPTER

# 9

# A WORD ABOUT RESILIENCE

*You may have to fight a battle more than once to win it.*
—MARGARET THATCHER

This is the chapter where we wrap up our time together. Our exploration of the transformational journey and why taking that journey is worth engaging in the difficult work that comes with it is coming to a close. But in many ways, we hope it's just the very beginning of the actual journey for you.

Maybe you've started that journey already, or maybe you've started and decided to "go back home," if you will. Maybe you're just now, for the first time in your life, realizing that this journey is available to you. To all of you in each of these situations, we invite you to embark on your journey today!

But make no mistake, this is NOT a journey for the faint of heart! It will require resilience. Earlier, we invited you to exhibit courage and grit as you began to take a step forward. But we want to be really honest with you—this journey will require you to channel all the courage and grit you have if you are going to be resilient.

Here's how we think about resilience. It is "the capacity to withstand or to recover quickly from difficulties."[30]

I know what you're thinking because we thought it, too, when we were in your shoes. "Does that mean this journey is one that will include difficulties?" Yes. Yes, it does.

At the time of writing this, I (Kurt) have just finished watching one of the most epic journeys with my wife and kids! My wife and I had previously watched it, but our kids have just now seen the magic and wonder that is *The Lord of the Rings Trilogy*! (Yes, I know that they were books first, don't come at me, bro!)

And when I say "epic," I mean EPIC! If you haven't seen them, this is the story of two unexpected heroes making the journey of a lifetime to save the future of humankind—and Hobbitkind. And over the course of three movies and nine hours, we get to see the highest of highs and the lowest of lows of this incredible journey. The prevailing tone is, "I just can't do this anymore."

But through resilience none knew these heroes possessed, the journey came to its most favorable end despite the astronomical odds against them.

Your transformational journey might not take you to Mordor (that's a REALLY bad place, maybe the WORST and most dangerous place in *The Lord of the Rings*), and it may not take you to the literal ends of your physical and emotional capabilities. But it also might.

> **To get different results in our lives, we need to try different things.**

What we believe to be true is that it will be challenging, mostly because it will take us to places we either intentionally or unintentionally have not gone before, or at least not gone willingly before. As we've said before, to get different results in our lives, we need to try different things, which means going to those places and encounters we've avoided to this point in our lives.

---

[30] "Resilience," Oxford Dictionary.

There are reasons why resilience is required and why this journey can be incredibly difficult at times.

First, the practice of self-discovery for the purpose of growing self-awareness can unearth all sorts of things, some expected and some unexpected. One friend I've walked with through some of this work used to say: "I'm pretty nervous about digging into the encounters in my past because I just don't know what I'm going to find. I also don't know if I'll be able to shut off the flow of discovery once it starts." Sara, we'll call her, compared this fear to the experience of opening one of those old-fashioned toys that looked like a normal can, but when you unscrewed the lid, a bunch of springy "snakes" popped out at you.

Sara, rightfully and validly, named her fear. She is afraid that once the "snakes" began popping out, there would be no way to control it. She's right, at least with the toy, in saying that once the lid is opened, they're all coming out!

While this analogy may be helpful, we also believe it breaks down a bit.

There is certainly the chance that the "snakes" of self-discovery will come out of the can all at once. But we also believe that Sara—and you—CAN put the lid back on the snake jar before all the snakes come out.

How? It seems like a good first step to acknowledge the potential risk of the snakes coming out. Knowing the risk the snakes might pose and taking intentional steps to create ways to push the pause button when self-discovery feels too heavy can create a necessary sort of relief valve to keep us safe and well.

Maybe it's taking a "step away" from the work for a day or two. It's okay to take a break. Because this work can be challenging, it is expected (and completely okay) that you will need a break here and there.

Remember, the journey is a marathon, not a sprint. The goal of this journey isn't to sprint through the finish line if you will. The goal is to become more whole and to experience real transformation in all parts of your life!

Another step you can take is to share what you're finding with a trusted friend. It is good to not carry the weight alone. Maybe it's a session with your counselor or therapist. Whatever you find helpful, resilience will help you get back into the work of self-discovery and back on the journey toward transformation.

But there's another challenge that comes to mind that will require us to exercise resilience. At BCG, we say this work of transformation will "change the dance."

You have likely lived the life you live for a long time. We both would say it like this: We lived as our false selves. We hid and tried to "fake it til we make it" for most of our adult lives. Remember, most of us think that's just what it means to be an adult in the West. We get used to it. We get used to the impact on us.

So does everyone around us! If you are a self-deferring people pleaser, the people you spend your life around have become accustomed to that too. If you show up in your family system today the same way you did when you and your siblings were children, your family system knows how you will show up and behave. If you sit in important meetings within the organization you work for and simply stay quiet, never voicing hard opinions, those people around the table expect that you'll always do so.

You'll notice that those ways of being that the systems around you have come to know from you might not be aligned with your truest self or the way that you'd prefer to show up in the world. The work of transformation will always mean new patterns of behavior and new ways of being.

But as Jim Herrington and Trisha Taylor have taught us pertaining to systems thinking, when our patterns of behavior and the ways we show up change in those systems, anxiety ensues. The systems and the people in those systems will do everything they can to keep the systems in place as they've been.

That means that when the self-deferring people pleaser begins to assert themselves, the system will be upset. When you begin to show up in your family of origin as your true self instead of as your ten-year-old self, the members of your family will seek to get you back to acting like your ten-year-old self. And when you start to name challenging (and true) views and opinions at work, your colleagues will seek to get the quiet version of you back.

It's probably a safe bet that you, reader, have been to a wedding reception as an adult. If you stay long enough for the dance to start, you know there is ALWAYS a time when the DJ will play a song that has a coordinated dance. "The Electric Slide," "The Cupid Shuffle," or "The Chicken Dance." You know the ones.

Now imagine that you're out on the dance floor in the middle of a killer "Cupid Shuffle" with all your friends. But maybe it's not a perfect Cupid Shuffle. Maybe it's only pretty good. Now imagine another person (not sure why, but I imagine this person's name is Kyle) coming onto the dance floor and doing the most perfect Cupid Shuffle you've ever seen! It's quite beautiful, and you're stunned by its majesty! But just as quickly, you realize that your Cupid Shuffle is different, and everyone can see it. You have to do something because it's likely that your "standing out" is not an option in your mind.

In this wedding reception example, you have a couple of options. You COULD go up to Kyle and say, "Kyle, you do the most beautiful Cupid Shuffle I've ever seen! Teach me!" You also COULD leave the dance floor, going back to your seat to eat your way-too-small piece of wedding cake. Or you COULD try to get Kyle to do the same dance you're doing, the imperfect Cupid Shuffle, so that you won't stand out as the "weird one." OK, this is a silly example, but you see what happens in the illustration when Kyle changes the dance, quite literally.

In all seriousness, as you grow in your own wholeness and authenticity through the work we're inviting you to engage, you WILL be changing the dance, and people WILL try to get you to keep doing the dance you usually do.

But isn't the new dance better? Yes, yes, it is. But what's so hard about changing the dance is the potential for the change in relational dynamics. When systems experience change happening, people might withdraw from you, they might sabotage your work and growth, or they might just flat-out tell you to stop what you're doing.

Resistance to your new ways of being may surprise you, but it is not unexpected. It's actually quite normal. It probably indicates real growth and transformation. Resistance like that doesn't mean you should abandon the new ways of being you're trying on. It also doesn't mean that the people doing the resisting are bad. They're not; it just means they are human.

> **Resilience is the quality that allows you to feel the very real resistance and keep going.**

Resilience is the quality that allows you to feel the very real resistance and keep going.

But resilience doesn't just grow on trees, as they say. Nor do we just "will ourselves" to be resilient. Being resilient is a practice that we get to—practice. Doing hard things is hard. And like all things that are hard, if they were easy, we'd already be doing it. And if you're like most adults, you may feel some resistance in you to doing things as hard as practicing resilience in your transformational journey.

Allow us to offer you some tips to help grow your resilience:

- Keep your written purposeful and preferred promises with you, pulling them out often to remind yourselves of how you want to be as opposed to how your protective promise caused you to be.
- Remind yourself often of the exiled parts of you and welcome them into these places of challenge and difficulty along the transformational journey.
- Exercise emotional maturity, remembering that you get to decide which "dance" you do, not anyone else in your systems.
- Find someone to share what you're feeling as it pertains to resistance and resilience. Whether it's a trusted friend, a coach, or a

therapist, putting your feelings into words often allows a clearer perspective that can lead to greater resilience.

I think what we're saying, and how we want to wrap up on resilience, is that this is really hard work! There will likely be points along the way that you'll want to give up and just go back to "adulting" in ways you always have. You know what that requires, and you know how to manage it, but new ways are hard. We have felt that same thing in our journeys.

But don't give up! Rest when you have to, pause when you must, but be resilient. Keep going! While it may not always feel like it in the moment, wholeness and authenticity are always greater and more sustainable than those old ways of living!

# EPILOGUE

You've probably guessed it by now. We are extremely passionate about this work. But what is "this work"? Said simply, the work is the pleasure of walking with people as wise guides while they engage in the transformational journey.

At the Brimstone Coaching Group, we exist to help exhausted, frustrated, and overloaded leaders experience contentment, fulfillment, and wholeness where they live, work, and play.

That's not just website filler. It's the work that we've given our lives to because we believe deeply that this is the work that will do nothing less than change the world.

It's not hyperbole!

It's our hope and deep desire that your journey will continue well after you've put this book down. In fact, we believe it's in that work, in the coming years of your own work, where the most beautiful and meaningful fruit will come to bear.

So may the last encouragement and gentle invitation to you be the invitation to find a wise guide to help you engage in the journey and stay on the difficult path of transformation.

We would love to have the chance to connect with you! If you'd like to learn how we might serve you, please find us at www.brimstonecoachinggroup.com.

Whether you choose to work with us or not, even more than we want you to connect with BCG, we hope you will live a life of contentment, fulfillment, and wholeness. We believe it is best achieved with a coach, a counselor, or a therapist.

# ABOUT THE AUTHORS

Authors Kurt Bush and Chris Godfredsen first met at Western Theological Seminary at the outset of their graduate studies. After much parsing of Greek verbs together, the two began and continued their own journeys of self-discovery through a formation process called Faithwalking. Years before the launch of the Brimstone Coaching Group, Kurt and Chris partnered together to help Faithwalking participants see growth and transformation in their own lives. The two of them began working more closely together, coaching individuals and teams in the organizations they led.

After years of coaching and journeying with people in that way together but separately, Kurt and Chris began to dream of what it might be like to do more of this work together. That wondering morphed into Kurt inviting Chris to join in launching the Brimstone Coaching Group and continuing the work together more formally in January 2024. Since that time, the Brimstone Coaching Group has served individual leaders, corporate leadership teams, nonprofit boards, and even athletic teams in taking real and tangible steps toward transformation, leading to contentment, fulfillment, and wholeness. Kurt and Chris continue to give their lives to this work of transformation by helping clients work the Transformational Equation (Encounter + Reflection = Transformation) in order to see the world changed, one transformational journey at a time!

To engage more deeply with Kurt and Chris through the Brimstone Coaching Group, visit www.brimstonecoachinggroup.com to begin an initial conversation to see if BCG might be a good fit for you or your group.

They can also be found on most podcast platforms and YouTube on "The Brimstone Coaching Podcast," where they explore the many concepts and practical applications of the work they do with clients on a regular basis. Kurt and Chris are ready to partner with you and your team as you seek a life filled with more contentment, wholeness, and purpose.

www.ingramcontent.com/pod-product-compliance
Lightning Source LLC
LaVergne TN
LVHW061550070526
838199LV00077B/6981